AT MY TABLE

AT MY TABLE

MARY McCARTNEY

Vegetarian Feasts for Family and Friends

STERLING EPICURE

New York

STERLING EPICURE
New York

An Imprint of Sterling Publishing
1166 Avenue of the Americas
New York, NY 10036

First Sterling Epicure edition published in 2015

First published in Great Britain in 2015 by Chatto & Windus, Random House

ISBN 978-1-4549-1659-8

Distributed in Canada by Sterling Publishing
c/o Canadian Manda Group, 664 Annette Street
Toronto, Ontario, Canada M6S 2C8

For information about custom editions, special sales, and premium and corporate purchases,
please contact Sterling Special Sales at 800-805-5489 or specialsales@sterlingpublishing.com.

Manufactured in China

2 4 6 8 10 9 7 5 3 1

www.sterlingpublishing.com

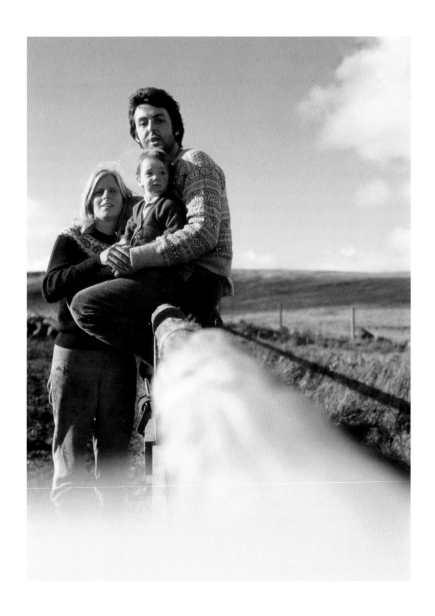

For my mum and dad, thank you for giving
me a passion for vegetarian cooking.

CONTENTS

INTRODUCTION

Hello. I'm back with my second book and lots more ideas, ingredients, and recipes that I'm really excited about. There are just so many great vegetarian options that I want to share with you.

When I was thinking about how to pull all these ideas together, I was struck by how important food is, in terms of my own memories, of those magical moments that stand out over the years. Sharing a meal with family and friends is an opportunity to relax together, to laugh together, and to bond together. Some of my happiest memories revolve around food, and I've tried to re-create those memories for my own children.

So what I decided to focus on for At Our Table *was specific occasions. For me, food is such an important part of turning an event into something special. The love and passion that you put into cooking for people is repaid with great conversation and an empty plate—and lasting memories.*

So if my first book, Food, *was about individual dishes, this book is about showing that you can create a variety of complete vegetarian menus to complement a range of very different occasions—my way of showing how flexible vegetarian cooking can be! I love to plan menus, as it allows you to find the context for each individual dish, and the challenge was to create entire meals that would be delicious and satisfying for meat eaters and vegetarians alike. The menu plans are designed to inspire, and to help take away the stress of cooking for others.*

When we were growing up as a vegetarian family, we never felt we were missing out at mealtimes. But time and again, I come up against the idea that, without meat, a meal—and certainly a special or celebratory meal—is not complete. I hope that this book will show that there are endless and exciting possibilities for meat-free cooking, and encourage many home cooks to try something new.

Of course I've added some photographs along the way to help tell the story.

Hope you enjoy.

Love, Mary

COOKING NOTES

KEY SYMBOLS:

GF = gluten-free or can be adapted to be gluten-free
V+ = vegan or can be adapted to be vegan
DF = dairy-free or can be adapted to be dairy-free

Since I wrote my last book I have modified the way I eat. I've become a lot more interested in the science of food because I wanted to expand my knowledge of how to eat well and prepare tasty and satisfying meals while maximizing the benefits to my health.

GLUTEN-FREE ALTERNATIVES

Gluten is the protein component found in grains such as wheat, rye, and barley and it's also found in some oats. With the increased awareness of the health problems caused by celiac disease and gluten sensitivity, there is now a good range of gluten-free alternatives available. I realized that I was eating a lot of gluten in my diet and it was starting to make me feel sluggish. After cutting back on gluten I felt more energetic and less bloated. So now, where I can, I always use gluten-free options and ingredients.

BUCKWHEAT FLOUR (alternative to wheat or spelt flour): Despite the name, buckwheat is not a cereal grain; it is a fruit seed that is related to the rhubarb family and sorrel. I use buckwheat flour as a gluten-free alternative to wheat flour as it acts as a binding agent in sauces and in recipes such as my Zucchini and Leek Fritters (p. 178), Gluten-Free Seeded Bread (p. 30), and in my cookies (see p. 134, 139, and 199). I like to use Doves Farm buckwheat flour (they also make a wide range of other gluten-free flours).

MASA HARINA CORN FLOUR: Masa, the Spanish word for "dough," is the traditional flour used to make corn tortillas. It is made with hominy, or dried corn kernels that have been soaked and cooked in lime water and then ground into masa.

MAIZE CORNMEAL FLOUR: Maize cornmeal flour is different from the purely starch, fine, white powder cornstarch, which is separated from the protein and other components of maize flour. Maize cornmeal flour is the entire corn kernel milled into flour, and it contains protein. The grind can vary from fine to coarse (also known as polenta).

GLUTEN-FREE FLOUR: Quite a few brands of gluten-free, all-purpose flour and pastry mix are now available in most supermarkets and health food stores, as well as online. Bob's Red Mill and Blends by Orly, for example, offer reliable gluten-free flour and gluten-free baking mixes.

GLUTEN-FREE PASTA: You can now find a wide variety of gluten-free pastas, made from rice, corn, quinoa, etc. My favorite variety is Doves Farm brown rice pasta.

TAMARI (alternative to soy sauce): Tamari is a liquid by-product of the fermentation process of miso. Tamari sauce is very similar in taste to soy sauce, and I like to use it to add flavor to recipes such as soups, gravy, roasts, and stews. Tamari is usually gluten-free (but it's best to double-check the brand you purchase), unlike soy sauce, which contains wheat. Tamari has less salt and is a good source of B3, manganese, and protein.

SUGAR CANE SWEETENER ALTERNATIVES

I have quite a sweet tooth, but try to moderate my sugar intake as I know too much isn't healthy. One thing I try to do is use different types of sugars that either have an added health benefit or have a lower glycemic index (a number associated with a food type that informs the food's effect on a person's blood sugar) than sugar cane, so I can avoid sugar spikes.

COCONUT SUGAR: I like to use coconut sugar as an alternative to cane sugar in recipes. It is made from the sap of the coconut palm, which is heated to evaporate the water and reduce it to granules. Coconut sugar is nutritious and has a lower glycemic index than sugar cane, which means it does not cause such sugar spikes and crashes. It has a similar taste to brown sugar with a bit of a caramel flavor too.

MAPLE SYRUP: Maple syrup is a natural sweetener made from the sap of certain varieties of maple trees. Check the label to make sure you buy pure maple syrup and not maple-flavored syrup. The latter is not pure, as it is often made using flavored refined sugar or high-fructose corn syrup. Pure maple syrup is pricey, but I think it's worth investing in as you can use it sparingly. It is very sweet and contains minerals such as manganese, magnesium, calcium, and potassium. I love it best lightly drizzled over pancakes.

AGAVE: Agave syrup is the sweet syrup produced from several species of the agave plant. It has a lower glycemic index than cane sugar and so causes less of a sugar spike. I like to use agave syrup instead of cane sugar to sweeten my Luxury Hot Chocolate (p. 200) and Caramel Dipping Sauce (p. 197). Agave is now available in many health-food shops and supermarkets.

HONEY: Honey has antioxidant and antibacterial properties. I keep a jar of runny honey in my store cupboard. Among many things, I like to use a little to stir into a tomato sauce to take away any acidity.

BLACKSTRAP MOLASSES: Molasses is a very dark, thick syrup that is a by-product of the sugar-refining process. It has a high mineral content and is a good source of iron. Molasses has a strong taste; to me it tastes a bit like licorice.

HEALTHY FATS

The types of fats we eat really matter. For years I avoided all fats, thinking they would make me overweight and unhealthy. The more I looked into it I realized there are a variety of good fats that are really important to eat—monounsaturated fats, polyunsaturated fats, and omega-3 fatty acids—as they help to protect our overall physical and emotional health. So now I make sure I include a good range of "good" fats in my meals.

There are fats that are best avoided as they can have a negative effect on health. These are trans fats and saturated fats, which are reported to be unhealthy and can increase your "bad" cholesterol levels.

GOOD MONOUNSATURATED FATS: avocados; olive oil; sunflower oil; sesame oil; olives; and nuts such as almonds, peanuts, macadamias, hazelnuts, and cashews.

GOOD POLYUNSATURATED FATS: walnuts; pine nuts; and seeds such as sesame, sunflower, pumpkin, and flax.

SOURCES OF OMEGA-3 FATTY ACIDS: flaxseed oil, hemp seed oil, walnut oil, and omega seed mix.

COOKING NOTES

DAIRY-FREE ALTERNATIVES

Since moderating the number of dairy products I eat I've discovered I have more energy. Also, growing numbers of people have found they are intolerant of or allergic to dairy. So I have worked a good variety of dairy-free alternatives into my everyday life. The good news is these are now more readily available than ever before.

ALMOND MILK: Almond milk is the dairy-free milk option I like to use most; it works well as a milk substitute in most aspects of cooking and I like its subtle flavor. I use it on breakfast cereals, in smoothies and when making my Quinoa Porridge (p. 45). It is also a good source of vitamin E and is gluten-free.

RICE MILK: Rice milk is a thinner milk alternative. It doesn't have many extra minerals and vitamins, so manufacturers often fortify it with extra calcium and vitamins. It is a good option if you have nut allergies and want gluten-free and low-fat alternatives.

SOY CREAM: I use soy cream as a dairy cream alternative. When using it in cooking, I heat it gently before adding to hot ingredients, as I find that way it doesn't curdle. It works well in soups instead of dairy cream, and is good poured over desserts.

COCONUT OIL: Virgin coconut oil is now available in good health-food shops and is a good alternative to butter when baking.

DAIRY-FREE CHEESE: I don't use much dairy-free cheese, as I've not found many that I enjoy eating. However, my local health-food shop recently introduced me to Daiya, which I do like, particularly their Cheddar flavor slices, and these are also suitable for vegans.

PROTEINS

As a vegetarian, I pay attention to the proteins I eat, as plant-based proteins are not generally complete proteins (which means no one source provides all the amino acids you require). So, while there are many good vegetarian sources of protein, I try to eat different combinations of proteins from vegetables, grains, beans, legumes, nuts, seeds, and eggs so I get a varied supply of protein sources in my diet. The added benefit is that most of these sources also provide a good amount of dietary fiber too.

QUINOA: Quinoa is a grain that is a complete protein as it contains all nine essential amino acids. It is also a good source of fiber and iron. I often cook up a batch of quinoa and keep it chilled in the fridge in an airtight container so I can add it to soups or salads as required. Also, I often use it instead of rice—it works well with my One-Pot Chili (p. 194) scooped on top to make a complete meal.

ORGANIC FREE-RANGE EGGS: For the recipes in this book that call for eggs I use organic free-range eggs, because they come from hens that are given organic feed and the hens are treated more humanely than caged hens as they are given outdoor space to roam around in. These eggs are a good source of amino acids, vitamins, and minerals.

BLACK BEANS: These are a good source of protein, fiber, and antioxidants.

CHICKPEAS: Chickpeas belong to the legume family and are good sources of protein, fiber, manganese, and folate.

LENTILS: A great source of protein, lentils can also help to lower cholesterol because they contain plenty of soluble fiber.

FAVA BEANS: Also known as broad beans, fava beans contain protein and provide a good supply of vitamin K, vitamin B6, potassium, folate, and fiber.

KIDNEY BEANS: These are a good source of protein, vitamin C, iron, folate, and dietary fiber.

CANNELLINI BEANS: Cannellini beans are a good source of protein, antioxidants, and copper.

FROZEN PEAS: As well as being a good source of protein and antioxidants, these have anti-inflammatory properties and provide good amounts of vitamins B1, B2, B3, and B6, and vitamin K.

BROWN RICE: Brown rice is a good source of selenium, manganese, antioxidants, and dietary fiber.

FIRM TOFU: This is a good source of amino acids, iron, and calcium.

ADDING FLAVOR

NUTRITIONAL YEAST FLAKES: I sometimes use a spoonful of Engevita nutritional yeast flakes (by Marigold) to add flavor to a recipe such as veggie burgers or a roast. It is an inactive yeast that is rich in B vitamins. It has a cheese-like flavor, although it is dairy-free.

MARIGOLD REDUCED-SALT VEGETABLE BOUILLON: This is my preferred vegetable bouillon, which I often use as a vegetable stock for soups, gravies, and in many other savory recipes. I prefer this reduced-salt version, as I find many stock cubes and bouillons can be too salty.

CELEBRATION

BRUNCH

CELEBRATION BRUNCH

I absolutely love brunch: Who wouldn't love a lazy late breakfast that you eat as the minutes tick toward lunchtime? On the weekend, I like to invite people over, buy the papers, and make a selection of food for us all to choose from. But sometimes a special occasion calls for something extra, so this menu has a few twists and added ingredients to make it that little bit more celebratory.

MENU

Indulgent Chive Scrambled Eggs - GF, DF

Honey Lime Fruit Salad - GF, V+, DF

Medley of Muffins - DF

Pomegranate and Orange Prosecco Cocktail - GF, V+, DF

Gluten-Free Seeded Bread - GF, V+, DF

INDULGENT CHIVE
SCRAMBLED EGGS

SERVES 1

Prep time: approx. 5 minutes
Cooking time: approx. 5 minutes
(slightly longer if you are cooking
for a large number of people)

INGREDIENTS

Per person:

2 large free range eggs
sea salt and freshly ground
 black pepper, to taste
1 tablespoon butter
 (or dairy-free alternative)
2 tablespoons milk or cream (or soy
 cream for a dairy-free option)
1 tablespoon finely chopped
 fresh chives

GF, DF

How do you take an unbeatable classic like scrambled eggs and elevate it to something special? I have taken my inspiration from France. Using a whisk instead of a wooden spoon makes the eggs light and fluffy, and adding a herb, in this case chives, finishes the job beautifully. I love the added flavor and the pretty flecks of green.

METHOD

Crack the eggs into a mixing bowl, season with a little salt and pepper, and beat with a hand whisk.

Melt the butter over medium heat in a saucepan large enough to accommodate the number of eggs you are preparing, with enough room to be able to stir without spillage.

When the butter is melted, add the well-beaten eggs to the pan and stir with a hand whisk—this will ensure the eggs maintain a light texture.

As soon as the eggs begin to set, add the milk or cream and the chopped chives. Continue to stir with the whisk until the eggs reach a creamy consistency.

Serve immediately on hot buttered toast.

HONEY LIME FRUIT SALAD

SERVES 6

Prep time: 10 minutes

INGREDIENTS

2 cups pineapple, peeled and cored

1 medium ripe mango, peeled and
   pit removed

2 kiwi fruit, peeled

1⅛ cups strawberries (approx.
   2 handfuls)

½ cup blueberries (approx.
   2 handfuls)

For the dressing:

2 tablespoons freshly squeezed lime
   juice (approx. 1 lime)

½–1 teaspoon finely grated fresh
   ginger, to taste

1 tablespoon honey (or agave syrup)

GF, V+, DF

For me, a brunch isn't complete without a great fruit salad. The color and fragrance it brings to the table is amazing and it's something everyone will dip into. In this recipe, I've added a dressing of honey, ginger, and fresh lime juice that brings extra punch to the salad.

METHOD

Chop the pineapple, mango, and kiwi into small bite-sized cubes and put them into a medium serving bowl.

Hull and quarter the strawberries and add them to the bowl, along with the blueberries.

Combine all the dressing ingredients in a glass or small bowl, mixing well until the honey dissolves into the lime. Pour the dressing over the chopped fruit and stir gently to allow the flavors to infuse. Set to one side until ready to serve.

This salad is delicious served with plain yogurt, chopped nuts, and an extra drizzle of honey, or you can simply enjoy it on its own.

MEDLEY OF MUFFINS

MAKES 12

Prep time: 15 minutes
Cooking time: 20–25 minutes

INGREDIENTS

For the basic muffin mix:

2 large free range eggs

½ cup vegetable oil

1 cup milk (or almond milk
   for a dairy-free option)

1 cup superfine sugar

3⅓ cups plain, whole-grain,
   or spelt flour

3 teaspoons baking powder

1 teaspoon salt

Pear and walnut muffin:

1 small pear, cored, peeled
   and finely chopped, mixed
   with ½ cup walnuts, finely
   chopped, and ½ teaspoon
   ground cinnamon

Berry muffin:

½ cup blueberries and/or raspberries

Lemon and poppy seed muffin:

zest of 1 lemon, juice of ½ lemon,
   and 1 teaspoon poppy seeds

DF

Freshly baked muffins are irresistible, but there are so many possible flavors—how do you choose? All my kids have a different favorite, of course. So, to get around the problem, I make a batch of the basic muffin mix, then divide the mixture into three separate bowls and add a different flavor to each bowl. These are our top three combinations, but you can play around and come up with your own.

METHOD

Preheat the oven to 375°F. Line a 12-cup muffin tin with muffin liners.

In a mixing bowl or food processor, beat the eggs and then mix in the oil, milk, and sugar. Sift in the dry ingredients and mix until well combined, but do not overbeat. Now that you have your basic muffin mix, you can get creative.

Divide the mixture equally between three bowls and add your preferred flavor ingredients. For instance, add the pear, walnuts, and cinnamon, to one, the mixed berries to another, and, finally, the lemon zest, lemon juice, and poppy seeds to the last one. Or come up with your own variations.

Spoon the mixture equally into the muffin liners—each bowl should have enough mixture for four muffins. As a rough guide, each muffin liner should be around three-quarters full.

Bake in the middle of the oven for 20-25 minutes, or until a skewer comes out clean.

POMEGRANATE AND ORANGE
PROSECCO COCKTAIL

SERVES 6
Prep time: 5 minutes

INGREDIENTS
1 750ml bottle Prosecco or
   Champagne or sparkling white wine
½ cup freshly squeezed orange juice
¾ cup pomegranate juice

6 champagne flutes

GF, V+, DF

I was introduced to Prosecco at a friend's house a few years ago and find it a lighter and more drinkable sparkling wine than Champagne. It's also great mixed with fresh fruit juice, and here I've chosen pomegranate and orange to give it a real zing for a brunch menu. (Of course you can use Champagne if you prefer.)

METHOD
Chill your Prosecco (or Champagne or sparkling wine) and the orange and pomegranate juices.

Pour the Prosecco into six champagne flutes first, filling each one about two-thirds full. Mix the orange and pomegranate juices together in a pitcher and use to top off each glass.

GLUTEN-FREE SEEDED BREAD

MAKES 1 LOAF
Prep time: 10 minutes
Resting time: 1½ hours
Cooking time: 30 minutes

INGREDIENTS
⅔ cup potato flour (starch)
¾ cup buckwheat flour
1 cup corn flour, plus more
    for dusting the pan
½ cup seeds (a mix of pumpkin
    seeds, sunflower seeds, pine nuts)
1½ teaspoons active dried yeast
1⅔ cups warm water
1 teaspoon salt
oil, for greasing the pan

GF, V+, DF

I love bread—in fact there are times when only bread will do. I love it toasted and I love it with eggs; I love it for sandwiches and I love it simply spread with hummus or butter. To cut down on my gluten intake, I have started making gluten-free bread at home. What I don't eat on the day of baking, I slice, wrap in foil, and keep in the freezer. Then it's there, ready sliced, so I can put it straight in the toaster whenever I feel the need to indulge.

METHOD
Pour the flours and seeds into a medium mixing bowl and set aside. Put the active dried yeast into a medium-large mixing bowl and pour the warm water over it. Stir until the yeast has fully dissolved.

Using a wooden spoon, mix the flours, seeds, and salt into the yeast and water mixture. It should be the consistency of plain yogurt; if not, you may need to add an extra tablespoon or so of water to achieve the right consistency. Cover the bowl with a clean dish towel and leave to rest in a warm place for 1 hour.

In the meantime, grease an 8 x 4-inch loaf pan and dust with corn flour (this is to the keep from sticking to the pan when turning it out after baking). Then pour the mixture into the prepared loaf pan, cover again with the dish towel, and allow it to rest for 30 more minutes.

Preheat the oven to 475°F. Pour a couple cups of water into a roasting pan and place the loaf pan into the roasting pan. Put the pan into the oven, and turn the temperature down to 425°F. Bake for 30 minutes, until golden and a skewer comes out clean.

Turn the loaf out of the pan onto a wooden board and allow to cool. You will need to use a sharp bread knife to slice it, as the crust is quite crisp.

ENERGY

BREAKFAST

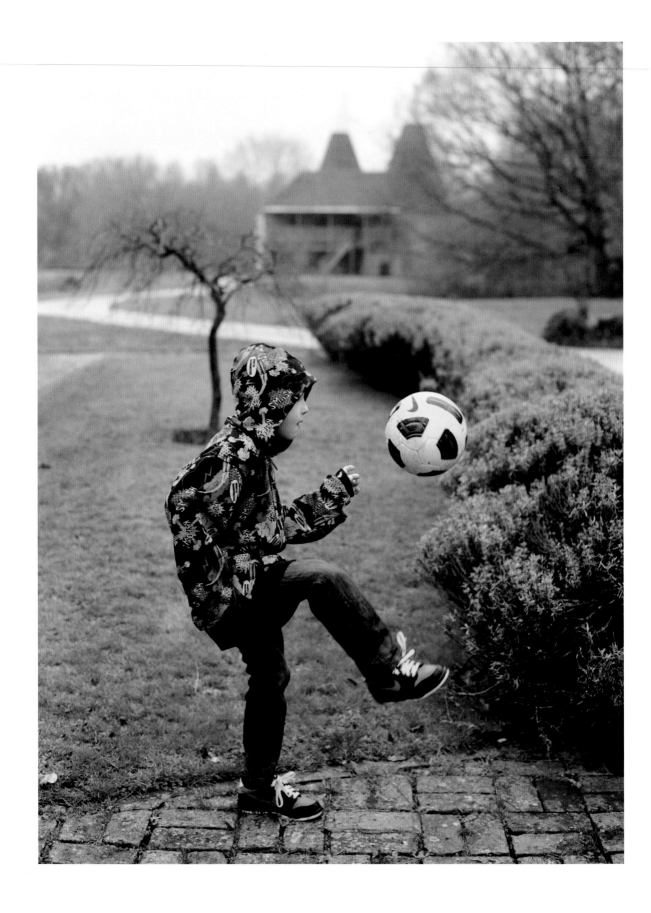

ENERGY BREAKFAST

For me, breakfast is the most important meal of the day. If I eat well in the morning, I'm set up for the day and much less likely to eat badly. So, here, I've created a menu that delivers on flavor and gives a powerful energy boost to kick off the day. You can choose one recipe from the menu each day, to keep your week varied, or make them all at once! Your choice.

MENU

Buckwheat Pancakes - GF, DF

Sliced Avocado and Soft-Boiled Eggs on Toast - GF, DF

Quinoa Porridge - GF, V+, DF

Energy Breakfast Smoothie - GF, V+, DF

BUCKWHEAT PANCAKES

MAKES 14–16 PANCAKES

approx. 3½ inches in diameter
(you can freeze any leftovers)

Prep time: 10 minutes

Cooking time: 10 minutes

INGREDIENTS

1 cup buckwheat flour

½ teaspoon baking soda

3 teaspoons baking powder

2 large free range eggs, separated

¾ cup milk (or almond or soy milk
   for dairy-free option)

1 tablespoon melted butter
   or coconut oil

3 teaspoons butter, or 2 teaspoons
   coconut oil, for frying

maple syrup, for drizzling on top

GF, DF

Buckwheat flour contains no gluten, although the name implies otherwise. Folding in the whisked egg whites ensures these pancakes retain a light taste and the maple syrup makes them irresistible. I usually serve four pancakes per person. If you are gluten intolerant, double check that your baking powder is gluten-free.

METHOD

Preheat the oven to 325°F. Prepare a cookie sheet with foil to wrap the pancakes in, and to keep them warm while you cook the rest of the batch.

Sift the buckwheat flour, baking soda, and baking powder together into a medium mixing bowl, and make a well in the center of the flour. Using a wooden spoon or hand whisk, mix the egg yolks and milk together in a medium bowl, and then gradually pour into the well of flour, beating all the time to avoid lumps. Stir in a tablespoon of melted butter or oil and continue to beat until your batter is a smooth, creamy consistency.

In a separate, medium mixing bowl, use a hand whisk or electric mixer to whisk the egg whites until they form soft peaks. Gently fold these whites into the batter, using a metal spoon and being careful not to beat all the air out of the mix; this will ensure light, fluffy pancakes.

Preheat a large, non-stick frying pan over a medium heat. Add a little butter or coconut oil to form a light glaze over the base of the pan. You can tell if it is hot enough to start cooking your pancakes by dropping a tiny amount of batter into the pan; if it sizzles, you are ready to go.

Pour the batter into the pan; 2 tablespoons per pancake, or if you have one on hand, a ¼-cup measuring cup is ideal. Depending on the size of your pan, you can probably cook in batches of three or four. But don't overcrowd your pan, as it will make it more difficult to flip the pancakes. When small bubbles start to appear on the surface of the pancakes, gently lift the edges with a spatula. If the underside is golden brown, flip them over and cook until the other side is golden too, and the pancakes are cooked through. Whenever the pan goes dry, add a little extra oil or butter and re-glaze the base before continuing. As you go, transfer the cooked pancakes to the cookie sheet, cover with foil, and place in the oven to keep warm until all the batter has been used up.

Serve the pancakes drizzled with maple syrup and maybe some fresh berries or chopped banana. If you have some pancakes left over, you can wrap them in foil and freeze them. Reheat from frozen, in a warm oven, as required.

SLICED AVOCADO AND
SOFT-BOILED EGGS ON TOAST

SERVES 2

Prep time: 10 minutes
Cooking time: 10 minutes

INGREDIENTS

2 large free range eggs
1 ripe avocado
juice of ½ lemon or 1 lime
¼ teaspoon red chili flakes or
   ½ teaspoon chopped and
   deseeded fresh red chili, or,
   if preferred, ½ teaspoon
   chopped fresh chives
2 slices of bread, such as multigrain,
   whole-grain or gluten-free
   (see recipe, p. 30)
butter or spread, for the toast
freshly ground black pepper
   and sea salt, to taste

GF, DF

I started to see avocado and egg on toast crop up quite often on restaurant and café menus. I didn't think I would like the combination, but when I tried it I loved it!

METHOD

For the soft-boiled eggs, fill a small saucepan with water and bring to a boil. Using a spoon, gently slide in the eggs and boil for 6 minutes. Turn off the heat, lift the eggs out with the spoon, and plunge into cold water for a couple seconds to stop further cooking and allow the eggs to cool enough so that you can peel off the shell.

Meanwhile, halve the avocado, remove the pit, and carefully scoop out the flesh. Slice each half thinly, and place on a plate. Lightly squeeze with lemon or lime juice and sprinkle with the chili or chives.

Now toast your bread and lightly butter it. Gently arrange half an avocado on top of each piece of toast. Peel the warm boiled eggs and lay one on top of each piece of avocado toast, breaking the egg in half with a knife to allow the yolk to spill out. Add a grind of black pepper and a sprinkle of sea salt. Ready to eat.

QUINOA PORRIDGE

SERVES 2

Prep time: 5 minutes
Cooking time: 20 minutes

INGREDIENTS

½ cup uncooked white quinoa, rinsed

1¼ cups milk (or unsweetened almond milk for dairy-free option; if using sweetened almond milk, there's no need for the 1 tablespoon of maple syrup/honey)

½ cup water

1 tablespoon maple syrup or honey, plus more for drizzling on top

½ teaspoon cinnamon

1 teaspoon vanilla extract

Ideas for toppings:

handful of fresh berries (raspberries, blueberries, strawberries)

chopped pear

chopped banana

chopped walnuts

hulled hemp seeds

GF, V+, DF

Porridge made with quinoa is a great alternative to traditional oats. There are many reasons why I like to use quinoa. It's a gluten-free grain, it's a complete protein, containing all nine essential amino acids, and it's a good source of iron, fiber, and magnesium. Used in this recipe, it also makes for a satisfying, energy-boosting breakfast.

METHOD

In a medium saucepan mix together the uncooked quinoa, milk, water, maple syrup, cinnamon, and vanilla extract.

Bring to a boil, then turn down the heat to low. Cover and simmer gently for about 20 minutes, stirring occasionally, until the quinoa has absorbed the milk and has the consistency of porridge. (If you prefer a thicker consistency, you can remove the lid and simmer for a few extra minutes.)

Divide between two bowls and drizzle with a little extra maple syrup or honey. Sprinkle with your desired toppings.

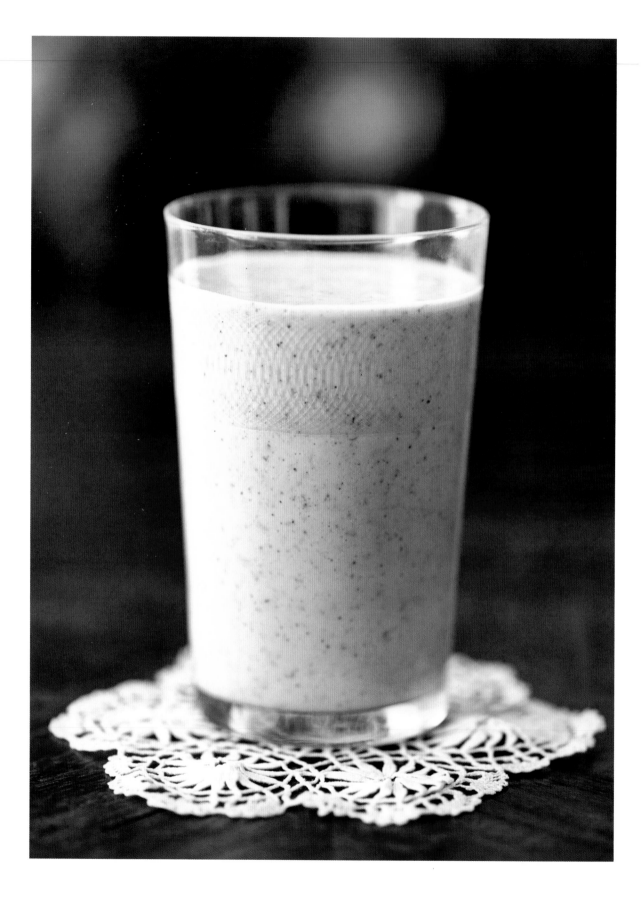

ENERGY BREAKFAST SMOOTHIE

SERVES 1

Prep time: 5 minutes

INGREDIENTS

¾ cup almond milk, rice milk,
  or dairy milk

½ tablespoon pumpkin seeds

1 tablespoon hemp seeds

1 tablespoon pine nuts

1 ripe banana

1 kiwi, peeled and chopped (optional)

1 scoop whey or protein powder

GF, V+, DF

The mornings can be such a rush, so I find the best way to take on board many of the nutrients I need to get through the day is to have a quick smoothie for breakfast. You can jam in all the healthy stuff and make it super-tasty, too. In this recipe I use pine nuts, because they have so many health benefits, being rich in essential minerals and vitamins and monounsaturated fatty acids. (I keep a little pack of pine nuts in my handbag to snack on throughout the day, too.) I also add protein to my smoothie to make it a complete breakfast. There are many powdered proteins available, from whey to hemp, but I usually use a non-dairy option called Spiru-Tein.

METHOD

For the quick version, put all the ingredients into a blender and blend until smooth—about 20-30 seconds.

However, if you have time the night before, pop the seeds and pine nuts into your milk and leave in the fridge overnight. Peel and chop the banana and keep it in the freezer overnight. Soaking the seeds and nuts will cause them to swell and soften, making them easier to digest. Frozen banana creates a much creamier, colder smoothie.

At breakfast time, add the chopped kiwi—and the protein, if using—to all the prepared ingredients in the blender and go!

MIDDLE EASTERN

FEAST

MIDDLE EASTERN FEAST

For 4–6

There are two reasons why I have a real passion for Middle Eastern food. Firstly, there are just so many great vegetarian options that I keep going back to again and again. Secondly, my father-in-law (who, unfortunately, I never met) was Lebanese, so this menu plan is dedicated to his memory.

MENU

Hummus - GF, V+, DF

Baba Ghanoush - GF, V+, DF

Tabbhouleh - GF, V+, DF

Falafel - GF, V+, DF

Lentils and Rice with Caramelized Onions - GF, V+, DF

Loubieh Bel Zeit (Green Beans in Tomato Sauce) - GF, V+, DF

Moussaka - GF

Nutty Baklava

HUMMUS

SERVES 4–6
Prep time: 5 minutes

INGREDIENTS
1 14-ounce can chickpeas

4 tablespoons sunflower
or extra-virgin olive oil

3 tablespoons tahini paste

4 tablespoons freshly squeezed
lemon juice (approx. 2 lemons)

2 small cloves garlic, peeled

½ teaspoon sea salt

2 tablespoons water

To garnish (optional):
extra-virgin olive oil
lightly toasted pine nuts
paprika
chopped fresh parsley

GF, V+, DF

Hummus is a staple in my family and we all love it—in sandwiches, on toast, scooped up with chips or vegetable sticks. Whichever way you choose to serve it, it tastes so good! It's easy to make and healthy, and you can always add your own twist to this recipe by blending in a spoonful of pumpkin seeds, sun-dried tomato, avocado, or whatever takes your fancy. It's packed with nutrients too, being a good source of protein, fiber, and healthy essential fats.

METHOD
Drain the chickpeas and rinse them briefly under cold running water. Put the chickpeas into a food processor. Add the oil, tahini paste, lemon juice, garlic, sea salt, and water.

Process for about 1 minute until smooth and creamy.

For a delicious finishing touch, if you like, drizzle with extra-virgin olive oil and top with a scattering of toasted pine nuts, a light dusting of paprika, or some freshly chopped parsley.

BABA GHANOUSH

SERVES 4
Prep time: 10 minutes
Cooking time: 40–45 minutes

INGREDIENTS

2 large eggplants (approx. 1⅓ pounds)
2 cloves garlic, finely chopped
pinch sea salt, or to taste
¼ teaspoon smoked paprika
2 tablespoons freshly squeezed
   lemon juice (approx. 1 lemon)
2 tablespoons tahini paste,
   or more to taste

To garnish (optional):
extra-virgin olive oil
fresh pomegranate seeds
chopped mint leaves

GF, V+, DF

This smoky-flavored dip is made up of roasted eggplant mixed with tahini, lemon juice, and garlic. I love it served alongside bowls of vegetable sticks and toasted pitas or flatbread, ready for scooping it up.

METHOD

Preheat the broiler. Place the eggplant directly on a baking sheet and grill them, turning every 5 minutes until the skins are charred and black all over. (Alternatively, if you have a gas cooktop or are having a summer barbecue, hold the eggplant with metal tongs over the open flame, turning them regularly, for about 5 minutes, until the skin is charred and blistered. This will give an extra smoky flavor to the finished dish. Then place on a baking sheet.)

Preheat the oven to 400°F. Place the baking sheet in the center of the oven and bake the eggplant for 40 minutes, until they are soft and cooked through.

Remove from the oven and allow to cool. Then cut open the eggplant and scoop the flesh into a colander or sieve, allowing any extra juices to drain away. Put the eggplant filling into a food processor or medium bowl.

Add the chopped garlic, sea salt, smoked paprika, lemon juice, and tahini paste and process in the food processor for about 5 seconds. Or mash by hand with a fork until you achieve a smooth consistency.

Serve just as it is, or with a drizzle of extra-virgin olive oil, some fresh pomegranate seeds, and a few chopped fresh mint leaves sprinkled on top.

TABBHOULEH

SERVES 4

Prep time: 15 minutes

Standing time: 10 minutes

Cooking time: 15 minutes

INGREDIENTS

⅔ cup uncooked white quinoa
   (for gluten-free option), rinsed,
   or bulgur wheat

¾ cup water

3 medium ripe red tomatoes,
   deseeded and diced

3 scallions, finely chopped

1⅛ cups cucumber (approx.
   ½ cucumber), diced

1⅔ cups fresh flat-leaf parsley,
   finely chopped

3 tablespoons finely chopped fresh
   mint (small handful)

sea salt and freshly ground black
   pepper, to taste

For the dressing:

4 tablespoons extra-virgin olive oil

3 tablespoons freshly squeezed
   lemon juice (approx. 1½ lemons)

pinch sea salt

GF, V+, DF

This refreshing salad combines lots of chopped fresh parsley and vibrant, ripe tomatoes with a tangy citrus lemon dressing. Traditionally it's made with bulgur wheat, but I like to use cooked quinoa instead, since I think it works well, and has the added advantage of being a gluten-free superfood.

METHOD

Place the quinoa (or bulgur wheat) in a medium saucepan, then cover with the water. Bring to a boil, cook for 15 minutes, then take off the heat and cover with a dish towel to absorb the steam. Allow to stand for 10 minutes. Remove the dish towel and fork through—the quinoa should be light with the grains separated. Allow to cool.

Meanwhile, put the tomatoes, scallions, and cucumber into a large mixing bowl.

Mix the dressing ingredients in a cup or small bowl and whisk with a fork for a few seconds until smooth.

When ready to serve, add cooled quinoa and the chopped herbs into the large bowl with the tomatoes, scallions, and cucumber. Pour over the dressing, season with salt and pepper, and toss well.

FALAFEL

MAKES APPROX. 10 FALAFEL

Prep time: 15 minutes

Chilling time: 1 hour

Cooking time: 10 minutes

INGREDIENTS

1 tablespoon vegetable oil

1 small onion, finely chopped

1 clove garlic, finely chopped

⅔ cup canned chickpeas, drained
and rinsed

⅔ cup fresh or frozen fava beans,
defrosted if frozen

1 scallion, finely chopped

2 tablespoons finely chopped fresh
parsley or cilantro

1 teaspoon ground cumin

1 teaspoon ground turmeric

1 teaspoon sea salt

½ teaspoon cayenne pepper

flour (plain or buckwheat), for dusting

vegetable oil, for frying

GF, V+, DF

This falafel is made using a mixture of blended chickpeas and broad beans, flavored with delicate spices and herbs. It is packed with protein and so versatile—try it with dips such as hummus, or stuffed into pita bread with some crisp salad leaves tossed in a lemon tahini dressing. The list goes on... I always make extra to snack on throughout the week.

METHOD

Heat 1 tablespoon of vegetable oil in a large pan and fry the onion and garlic over medium heat for 3-4 minutes, or until softened, then remove from the heat.

Add the onion and garlic to a food processor and add the chickpeas, beans, scallion, herbs, spices, and seasoning. Pulse until well combined and chopped fine. (If you don't have a food processor, just chop everything together very small.) Take 1 heaping tablespoon of the falafel mixture at a time and, using your hands (rinsed in cold water), shape into balls, flattening each one slightly to make a patty shape. You should be able to make about 10 balls out of this amount. Chill in the fridge for 1 hour.

When ready to cook, transfer the falafel to a chopping board and lightly dust all over with flour.

Pour enough vegetable oil into a deep frying pan so the oil is about ⅛ inch deep, and heat until it is hot. To test if it's hot enough, add a small drop of the mixture to the pan and if it sizzles, the oil is ready.

Fry the falafel (you may need to do this in batches) for about 1 minute on each side, until golden. Remove and drain on kitchen paper and repeat until all the falafel are cooked.

Good served with Hummus (p. 54) or salad.

LENTILS AND RICE
WITH CARAMELIZED ONIONS

SERVES 4

Prep time: 15 minutes

Cooking time: 30–45 minutes,
    depending on rice cooking time

INGREDIENTS

½ cup brown rice

1 cup hot vegetable stock

¾ cup dried green lentils, rinsed

2 tablespoons light olive oil
    or vegetable oil

3 medium onions (or 2 red onions
    and 1 white onion), halved and
    thinly sliced

1 teaspoon ground cumin

¼ teaspoon ground cinnamon

2 tablespoons chopped fresh parsley

pinch sea salt and freshly ground
    black pepper, to taste

squeeze of fresh lemon juice

GF, V+, DF

This lentil and rice mixture is mildly flavored with cumin and topped with sweet, caramelized onions. Its delicate flavor forms the perfect complement to the juicy tomato sauce in the Loubieh Bel Zeit (p. 65).

METHOD

Place the rice in a medium saucepan and pour in the hot vegetable stock. Bring to a boil and then turn down to a gentle bubbling simmer. Cover with a lid and cook for 25–40 minutes according to the instructions on the package. All of the liquid will be absorbed and the rice should be just tender (add more stock as required until the rice is cooked through). Then remove the lid, turn off the heat, and cover with a dish towel to absorb the steam.

While the rice is cooking, put the lentils into a medium saucepan and pour in enough water to cover them by 1 inch. Bring to a boil, then turn the heat down to a gentle simmer and allow the lentils to cook for about 15–20 minutes, until just cooked through. Drain in a sieve and set aside.

Meanwhile, heat the oil in a medium-large frying pan. Add the sliced onions, cumin, and cinnamon. Cook over medium heat, stirring often, for about 15–20 minutes, until the onions are caramelized, slightly crispy, and darker in color.

When the rice is ready, gently stir in the lentils, chopped parsley, and two-thirds of the cooked onions, reserving the rest for the garnish. Stir gently and season with a little sea salt and freshly ground black pepper to taste. Top with the remaining onions, and a squeeze of lemon juice, and serve.

LOUBIEH BEL ZEIT
(GREEN BEANS IN TOMATO SAUCE)

SERVES 4

Prep time: 10 minutes

Cooking time: 30 minutes

INGREDIENTS

2¾ cups ripe tomatoes, skinned and chopped (see right), or 1⅔ cups canned chopped tomatoes

2 tablespoons olive oil

4½ cups green beans, trimmed

2 medium onions, finely chopped

4 cloves garlic, finely chopped

1 tablespoon tomato purée

½ tablespoon grated fresh ginger

¼ teaspoon ground cinnamon

¼ teaspoon ground coriander

¾ cup water

sea salt and freshly ground black pepper, to taste

GF, V+, DF

An all-time favorite! Fresh green beans cooked in a deliciously simple tomato sauce. This dish makes a great accompaniment to the Lentils and Rice with Caramelized Onions (p. 63).

METHOD

To skin fresh tomatoes, prick them with a fork and plunge them into a pot of boiling water for about 5 minutes, or until the skin starts to split. Remove the tomatoes with a spoon and allow to cool before peeling off the outer skin and chopping finely.

Heat 1 tablespoon of the olive oil in a medium-large frying pan and fry the green beans gently for about 2 minutes on low-medium heat. Transfer the beans to a plate and set aside.

Meanwhile heat the remaining tablespoon of oil in the frying pan. Add the chopped tomatoes and onions, sauté gently for 5 minutes, then add the garlic, tomato purée, ginger, ground cinnamon, and coriander, and mix together well. Simmer gently for 10 minutes over low heat, stirring often.

Add the green beans to the tomato mixture; cover and simmer gently for 15 minutes. Season with a pinch of sea salt and freshly ground black pepper to taste. This can be eaten warm or, more traditionally, at room temperature.

MOUSSAKA

SERVES 6

Prep time: 45 minutes

Cooking time: 30–40 minutes

INGREDIENTS

4 tablespoons olive oil

2 medium onions, halved and
  thinly sliced

1 ⅓ cups mushrooms, thinly sliced

2 cloves garlic, finely chopped

1 tablespoon tamari (for gluten-free
  option) or soy sauce

¾ cup red wine

1 ⅔ cups canned chopped tomatoes

¾ cup canned chickpeas, drained
  and rinsed

¾ cup canned green lentils, drained
  and rinsed

2 bay leaves

sea salt and freshly ground black
  pepper, to taste

2 large potatoes (approx. 1 ⅛ pounds)

2 large eggplants (approx. 1 ⅓ pounds)

2 tablespoons chopped fresh herbs,
  such as parsley and thyme, or
  2 teaspoons dried mixed herbs

For the sauce:

3 ½ tablespoons butter or vegetable oil

½ cup buckwheat flour (for gluten-
  free option) or plain or spelt flour

2 ½ cups milk

1 ⅓ cups aged Cheddar, grated

⅔ cup feta cheese

¼ teaspoon nutmeg

freshly ground black pepper

2 large free range eggs, beaten

GF

This vegetarian version of the classic recipe gets great feedback from both vegetarians and meat eaters alike. It is hearty, warming, and satisfying.

METHOD

Preheat the oven to 350°F and lightly oil an 11 x 7-inch ovenproof dish or non-stick roasting tray.

In a medium saucepan, heat 2 tablespoons of the olive oil, then add the sliced onions and sauté for a couple minutes. Add the mushrooms, garlic, and tamari (or soy sauce) and allow to cook gently for 10 minutes, stirring often.

Stir in the wine and simmer for 1 minute to allow the alcohol to cook off. Add the tomatoes, chickpeas, lentils, and bay leaves; stir well and season with salt and pepper. Simmer for 20 minutes, adding a little water—around 2 tablespoons at a time—if the sauce gets too thick.

Meanwhile, cut the potatoes into rounds about ⅓ inch thick. Put into a medium pot of cold water, bring to a boil, and parboil them for 10 minutes—then drain.

Prepare the eggplant by trimming off the woody ends and then slicing into approximately ⅓-inch-thick rounds. Lay the potatoes and sliced eggplant on two greased non-stick baking trays, brush them with the remaining oil, and sprinkle with the herbs. Bake for about 30 minutes, turning them once halfway through cooking, until golden.

Now turn to your white sauce. Melt the butter (or oil) in a medium saucepan over low heat. Add the flour, stirring with a wooden spoon, to form a paste. Take the pan off the heat and gradually add the milk, a little at a time, stirring with a whisk to keep the sauce smooth and lump-free. Put the pan back over medium heat, bring to a gentle simmer, and cook for 2–4 minutes, stirring continuously, until the sauce has thickened. Add two-thirds of the grated Cheddar and crumble in the feta cheese, then stir until the cheese has melted. Add the nutmeg and freshly ground black pepper to taste and allow to cool slightly before finally beating in the eggs.

To assemble: Pour half the tomato sauce into the prepared ovenproof dish, followed by a generous layer of roasted potatoes and eggplant (about half the vegetables). Repeat with another layer of tomato sauce and the rest of the vegetable slices. Top with the white sauce and sprinkle with the remaining grated cheese. Bake for 30-40 minutes until golden and bubbly.

NUTTY BAKLAVA

MAKES 48 PIECES

Prep time: 30 minutes

Cooking time: 35–40 minutes

Cooling and setting time: 4–6 hours

INGREDIENTS

2 cups mixed nuts (almonds, walnuts, pistachios, or a combination of your favorite nuts)

¼ cup dark brown sugar, packed

½ teaspoon ground cinnamon

¼ teaspoon ground cloves

¼ teaspoon ground cardamom

1⅓ sticks butter

8¾ ounces store-bought filo pastry sheets

1–2 tablespoons finely chopped pistachios, for sprinkling on top

For the syrup:

1 cinnamon stick

½ cup dark brown sugar, packed

1 tablespoon fresh lemon juice (approx. ½ lemon)

5 tablespoons honey

½ cup water

I can't resist these bite-sized, indulgent, sweet pastries. They're made using layers of filo pastry, chopped nuts, and a gorgeous sticky, sweet syrup poured over them. The perfect end to a wonderful Middle Eastern feast.

METHOD

Preheat the oven to 350°F and lightly grease a baking tray (about 11 x 17 inches). Chop the nuts into small pieces, either using a large knife or by pulsing in a food processor, being very careful not to grind them to dust. Put the nuts in a medium mixing bowl. Mix in the sugar, cinnamon, ground cloves, and cardamom. Melt the butter in a small pan over a low heat.

Unwrap filo sheets and cut them to fit the baking tray—most commercial brands are 9 x 14 inches and contain 40 sheets per 16-ounce box, so you can simply cut them in half. Cover your pastry sheets with a lightly dampened, clean dish towel to prevent the pastry from drying out while you work. Place one sheet of filo pastry on the baking tray and, using a pastry brush, brush with melted butter. Repeat until your pile of pastry is eight sheets thick, each sheet brushed with butter. Spoon on half of the nut mixture and spread evenly over the prepared filo pastry. Cover with two more sheets of filo, brushing each one with butter.

Now spoon the other half of the nut mixture on top, and then top with another eight filo sheets, again ensuring that each sheet is brushed with the melted butter. Cut into 1-inch squares, using a sharp knife—this size baking tray should hold approximately 48. Bake for 35-40 minutes until lightly golden brown and slightly crisp.

While your baklava is cooking, make the syrup. Put all the syrup ingredients into a small saucepan. Bring to the boil, then reduce to medium-low heat and simmer for about 7 minutes, until slightly thickened and reduced. Remove the cinnamon stick and allow to cool.

Once the baklava is cooked, take it out of the oven and, while it is still hot, spoon the cooled syrup along the cut lines between the squares. Use every last drop. Sprinkle the chopped pistachios over the top while it is still sticky with syrup. Leave for 4-6 hours to cool and set. You'll be amazed how quickly 48 squares of this yummy treat will disappear.

MY AMERICAN SIDE

(BBQ) FEAST

MY AMERICAN SIDE

As my dad's from Liverpool and my mum was from America, I grew up telling anyone who asked where I was from that I was half American and half Liverpudlian. Mum was the main cook in our home, and my cooking style is influenced and inspired by her. This menu is based on what we would make for a barbecue at home. As a vegetarian family, we never liked to feel we were missing out by not eating meat. Traditionally, Dad is in charge of the barbecue when we make this wonderful feast.

MENU

Black Bean Burgers - GF, V+, DF

Thousand Island Dressing - GF, V+, DF

Eggless Mayonnaise - GF, V+, DF

Creamy Dill Potato Salad - GF, V+, DF

Chuck It In Chef's Salad - GF, V+, DF

Sweet Potato Oven Fries - GF, V+, DF

Corn on the Cob with Savory Parsley Butter - GF, V+, DF

Key Lime and Coconut Pie - GF

BLACK BEAN BURGERS

MAKES 6 BURGERS

approx. 1 inch thick and 3 inches wide

Prep time: 20–30 minutes

Chilling time: 1 hour minimum

Cooking time: 5–10 minutes

INGREDIENTS

1 14-ounce can black beans or
   kidney beans, drained

2 tablespoons light olive oil,
   or 2¼ tablespoons butter

1 medium red onion, finely chopped

1⅔ cups mushrooms, finely chopped

2 tablespoons tamari (for gluten-free
   option) or soy sauce

1 clove garlic, finely chopped

1 tablespoon chopped fresh parsley,
   or 1 teaspoon dried mixed herbs

1 scallion, finely chopped

½ teaspoon chili flakes (optional)

4 tablespoons buckwheat flour
   (for gluten-free option) or plain
   or spelt flour

1 tablespoon nutritional yeast flakes

freshly ground black pepper, to taste

3 tablespoons vegetable oil (if not
   cooking on the grill), for frying

GF, V+, DF

I make these burgers with black beans because they are packed with protein and fiber. If you don't have black beans, then kidney beans are a great alternative. I love them sandwiched between a burger bun with all the toppings—sliced pickles, tomato, onion, lettuce, melted cheese, Thousand Island dressing (or mayo and ketchup) and mustard. My advice is to never skimp on the toppings!

METHOD

Put the beans into a large bowl and roughly mash them with a potato masher, or blend them in a food processor for a few seconds. You want them to keep some texture, so do not over-mash.

Heat the olive oil (or butter) in a medium frying pan, then sauté the onion for 3 minutes. Add the mushrooms and tamari (or soy sauce) and fry for a few more minutes, until most of the mushroom juice has evaporated.

Stir in the garlic, herbs, scallion, chili flakes, and mashed beans, then allow the mixture to cook for about 2 minutes, stirring often. Transfer the mixture to a bowl and let cool slightly before mixing in the flour, nutritional yeast flakes, and black pepper to taste.

Divide the mixture into six portions and, using your hands, mold each portion into a patty shape (about 1 inch thick x 3 inches wide). Leave to chill in the fridge for at least 1 hour. To fry the burgers, heat the 3 tablespoons of vegetable oil in a medium-large frying pan and cook the burgers over medium heat for about 2 minutes on each side, or until cooked through.

If cooking on the grill, chill the burgers in the fridge or freeze them for a couple hours so they become firm. Then grill on both sides until golden brown and cooked through.

THOUSAND ISLAND DRESSING

SERVES 4
Prep time: 5 minutes

INGREDIENTS

4 tablespoons mayonnaise

1½ teaspoons tomato ketchup

1½ teaspoons tomato purée

1½ teaspoons capers or pickled
   gherkins, finely chopped

squeeze of fresh lemon juice
   (approx. 1 teaspoon)

small pinch sea salt and freshly
   ground black pepper, if desired

GF, V+, DF

This tangy dressing is great drizzled on top of the Black Bean Burgers (p. 76). But it's so versatile, I love to use it on salads and in sandwiches, too—it can help turn a simple cheese sandwich into a work of art! (Use the Eggless Mayonnaise below for a dairy-free dressing.)

METHOD

Mix all the ingredients together in a small serving bowl. This dressing is delicious spooned over veggie burgers or served as a dip with crudités. I also love it drizzled on leftover Festive Roast (p. 228) the next day. Any unused dressing can be stored in an airtight container in the fridge for up to 4 days.

EGGLESS MAYONNAISE

MAKES APPROX. 150ML
Prep time: 5 minutes

INGREDIENTS

½ cup sunflower oil

1 teaspoon Dijon or English mustard

1 tablespoon apple cider or white
   wine vinegar

2 tablespoons water

½ teaspoon sea salt

½ tablespoon ground/milled
   flaxseed (bought pre-ground)

GF, V+, DF

Let's face it, you can buy good-quality mayonnaise in most stores now. But sometimes it just feels more special to make your own. This mayo recipe leaves out the eggs and, instead, uses ground flaxseed, which I have in my pantry to add to smoothies for extra fiber and omega-3 benefits. I use this for dressings and in sandwiches, or just dolloped on the side of a baked potato with a big chopped salad.

METHOD

This technique uses an immersion stick blender. Pour the sunflower oil into a tall plastic pitcher or similar container, then add the mustard, vinegar, water, salt, and ground flaxseed. Take the stick blender and put it into the pitcher so that it sits firmly on the bottom. Start to whisk on a high speed (there is probably only one speed). This will create a vortex that will draw the oil down. It should thicken up within a few seconds, and once it has thickened you can move the hand whisk around to ensure that all the oil is blended. Serve or store in a sealed jar in the fridge, where it will keep for up to 1 week.

CREAMY DILL POTATO SALAD

SERVES 4–6
Prep time: 15 minutes
Cooking time: 15–20 minutes

INGREDIENTS
1⅓ pounds new potatoes
1 stick celery, finely chopped

For the dressing:
2 tablespoons mayonnaise
  or crème fraîche
2 tablespoons finely chopped fresh dill
1 scallion, finely chopped, or
  1 tablespoon finely chopped
  red onion
1 teaspoon Dijon whole-grain mustard
1 tablespoon chopped
  gherkins/cornichons
½ teaspoon freshly squeezed
  lemon juice
sea salt and freshly ground black
  pepper, to taste

GF, V+, DF

This potato salad is one of my barbecue favorites. It's creamy and satisfying, and the scallions and dill add a wonderful texture that makes it irresistible. It keeps well, so any leftover salad can be used the next day. To make this a vegan salad, use Eggless Mayonnaise (p. 79).

METHOD
Put the potatoes into a medium saucepan and cover with cold water. Bring to a boil, then turn down to a gentle simmer over low heat and cook for about 15–20 minutes or until just tender (test by pushing a knife into one of the potatoes—if it slips off, then it's done). Drain in a colander and let cool to room temperature.

To make the dressing, mix all the ingredients in a small bowl, seasoning with a small pinch of sea salt and black pepper to taste.

Put the cooled potatoes and chopped celery in a medium serving bowl and drizzle with the dressing. Mix until the potatoes are well coated. Chill the salad in fridge until ready to serve.

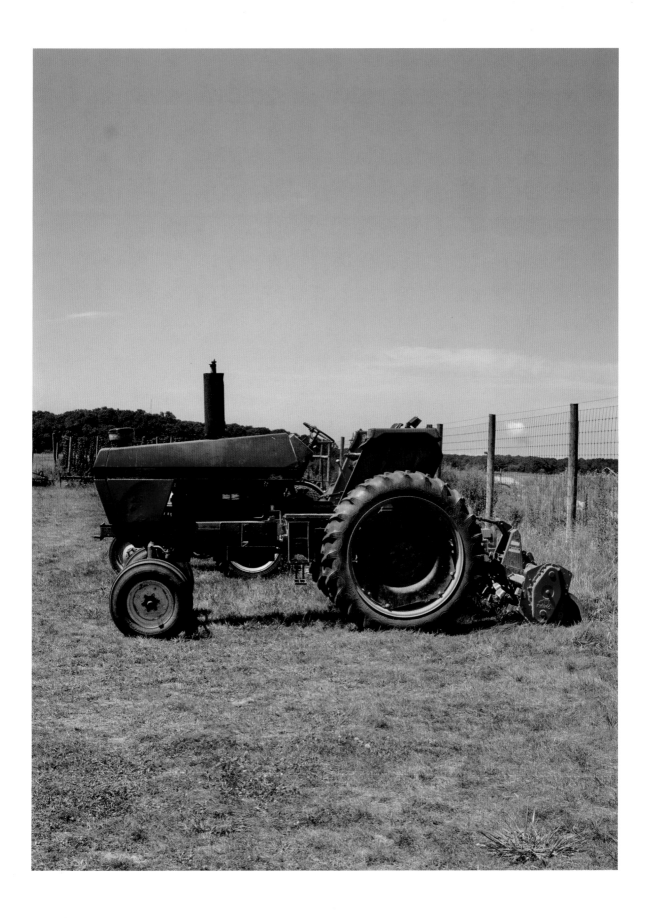

CHUCK IT IN CHEF'S SALAD

SERVES 4

Prep time: 15 minutes

INGREDIENTS

For the salad:

1 head baby gem lettuce, chopped
  into bite-sized pieces

2 cups watercress or arugula
  (large handful)

2 cups baby spinach leaves
  (large handful)

2 medium carrots, grated

2 scallions, finely chopped

¾ cup radishes, thinly sliced

For the dressing:

3 tablespoons extra-virgin olive oil

1½ teaspoons Dijon mustard

1 tablespoon white wine vinegar

1 tablespoon freshly squeezed lemon
  juice (approx. ½ lemon)

small pinch sea salt and freshly
  ground black pepper, to taste

GF, V+, DF

As a child growing up in England with an American mother, I had a surprise one day after school when I went home to my best friend's house for dinner. Her mother offered me a salad, which I expected to be like one of my mum's, with lots of crunchy ingredients tossed together in a huge salad bowl and served with a delicious dressing. What I got was a single wedge of tomato, a lettuce leaf, a chunk of cucumber, and some salad dressing poured over. It didn't quite have the wow factor of my mum's compositions. This salad is crisp and refreshing, and the colors make it look as good as it tastes.

METHOD

Put all the prepared salad ingredients in a large salad bowl. To make the dressing, whisk together all the ingredients in a small mixing bowl or mug.

Just before serving, drizzle the dressing over the salad and toss until evenly coated.

SWEET POTATO OVEN FRIES

SERVES 1 (multiply the quantities below to serve more)

Prep time: 5 minutes

Cooking time: 25–30 minutes

INGREDIENTS

Per person:

1½ teaspoons vegetable oil or sunflower oil, plus more for greasing the trays

1 sweet potato

¼ teaspoon sea salt

GF, V+, DF

Sweet potatoes give a little sweet caramelized twist to the usual fries, and you have the added benefit of extra vitamin A and beta-carotene. And they're cooked in the oven to keep the fat content low. Tasty and good for you—what more could you ask for?

METHOD

Preheat the oven to 400°F. Depending on how many people you are cooking for, coat the base of one or two baking trays lightly with a little oil.

Trim the ends off the potatoes. I leave the skin on, but peel now if preferred. Cut each sweet potato lengthways into medium-sized fries—around ⅓ inch thick is perfect—or cut into wedges if you prefer. Just make sure they are all a similar size so that they will cook evenly. Put the fries in a mixing bowl, pour in the oil and sea salt, and, using your hands, toss well until all the oil is evenly distributed.

Spread the uncooked fries evenly on the prepared trays, keeping them well spaced out. If they are overcrowded they tend to steam and become a bit soggy.

It's best to cook these fries on the top rack of the oven, but if you have prepared enough for two baking trays, then put one on the middle rack and one on the top. Swap the two trays around halfway through cooking. Turn the fries around a couple times during baking to ensure they cook evenly.

Bake for 25-30 minutes, or until golden brown and turning crisp. Serve immediately.

CORN ON THE COB
WITH SAVORY PARSLEY BUTTER

SERVES 4

Prep time: 10 minutes

Cooking time: 5 minutes

INGREDIENTS

4 ears of fresh, sweet corn on the cob

2⅛ tablespoons butter, margarine,
   or coconut oil, at room temperature

1 tablespoon chopped fresh parsley

1 tablespoon nutritional yeast flakes

GF, V+, DF

I like to brush savory parsley butter onto hot, freshly cooked corn on the cob. Nutritional yeast is a good source of B vitamins, and if you want to make this dish dairy-free, you can use a dairy-free spread instead of butter.

METHOD

If your corn cobs are not already husked, then prepare them by pulling off the outer leaves to expose the ears of corn. Strip off any of the silky threads still clinging to the cobs, then rinse under cold water.

To make the savory butter, mix the butter (or oil), chopped parsley, and nutritional yeast flakes in a small bowl, using a fork.

To cook the corn, bring a large pot of water to a boil—use enough water so that the corn will be completely submerged. Once the water is boiling, carefully place the corn in the pot and cook for around 3-4 minutes. Then remove the corn from the pot and drain on paper towels to get rid of the excess water.

Place a grill pan over medium-high heat until smoking hot. Add the corn and cook for a few minutes until charred, turning to cook on all sides. (Or, you could do this on a barbeque instead.)

While the corn is still hot, use a pastry brush to spread the softened butter mix evenly over it. Serve hot.

KEY LIME AND COCONUT PIE

SERVES 6–12 (6 very generous slices or 12 smaller slices)

Prep time: 15 minutes

Cooking time: 25–30 minutes

Cooling time: 20 minutes

Freezing/chilling time: 1 hour if freezing; 5 hours if chilling in fridge

INGREDIENTS

24 gluten free graham crackers (12 sheets)

½ cup coconut oil or butter, melted

¼ cup + 2 tablespoons desiccated coconut, packed

3 large free range eggs

1 14-ounce can condensed milk

juice of 5 limes (approx. ⅔ cup)

zest of 1 lime

½ cup coconut milk

GF

I grew up loving Key lime pie, but wanted to give it a little twist, so I experimented by adding coconut. This pie has a coconut-infused graham cracker base, topped with a lime and coconut creamy filling. Key limes are famously grown in Florida, but this recipe works just as well with the usual variety of limes that are widely available. I sometimes use gluten-free graham crackers to make this dessert gluten-free. Any leftovers can be left in the fridge.

METHOD

Preheat the oven to 325°F. Get out a 9-inch pie pan or loose-bottomed flan pan, about 1½ inches deep.

Blend the graham crackers into rough crumbs in a food processor (or bash them with a rolling pin in a freezer bag). Then put the cracker crumbs into a medium mixing bowl. Stir in the melted coconut oil or butter and the desiccated coconut. Press this mix into the base of your pie dish or flan pan and bake for 10 minutes.

Separate two of the eggs and put the egg yolks into a medium mixing bowl and the egg whites into a separate dry, clean medium bowl.

Add the third egg and the remaining ingredients to the bowl containing the egg yolks, and beat together well with a wooden spoon or hand whisk. Now, using a clean electric or hand whisk, whisk the egg whites to form soft firm peaks.

Gently fold the whisked egg whites into the coconut lime egg mixture so it is well combined. Pour this mixture evenly over the graham cracker base and bake for 15-20 minutes, until set on top but still slightly wobbly in the center.

Remove from the oven and let cool for 20 minutes. Then cover with plastic wrap and either freeze for a minimum of 1 hour or chill in the fridge for 5 hours (or preferably overnight) before serving. This will keep in the fridge for up to 3 days.

I HEART MEXICAN

FOOD

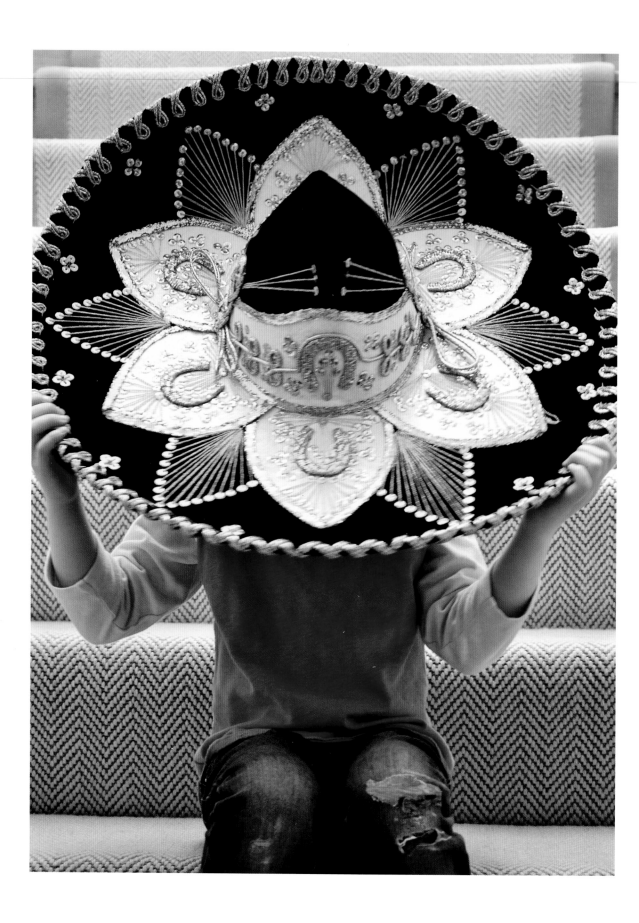

I HEART MEXICAN FOOD

For 4–6

As a family, we grew up loving Mexican food. I think it was all about the assembly: When we were kids we loved putting together the prepared ingredients for a great taco or tostada ourselves, always a mouthwatering process. Healthy ingredients, vibrant colors, and lots of variety make Mexican food a definite favorite for my family today.

MENU

Homemade Corn Tortillas - GF, V+, DF

Tostadas Deluxe - GF

Cornbread with Jalapeño and Sweet Corn Niblets

Mushroom and Cheese Quesadillas - GF

Mexican-Inspired Rice - GF, V+, DF

Avocado, Scallions, and Lime - GF, V+, DF

Mixed Peppers - GF, V+, DF

Cucumber and Watermelon Salad - GF, V+, DF

Dad's Margarita - GF, V+, DF

Mango Granita - GF, V+, DF

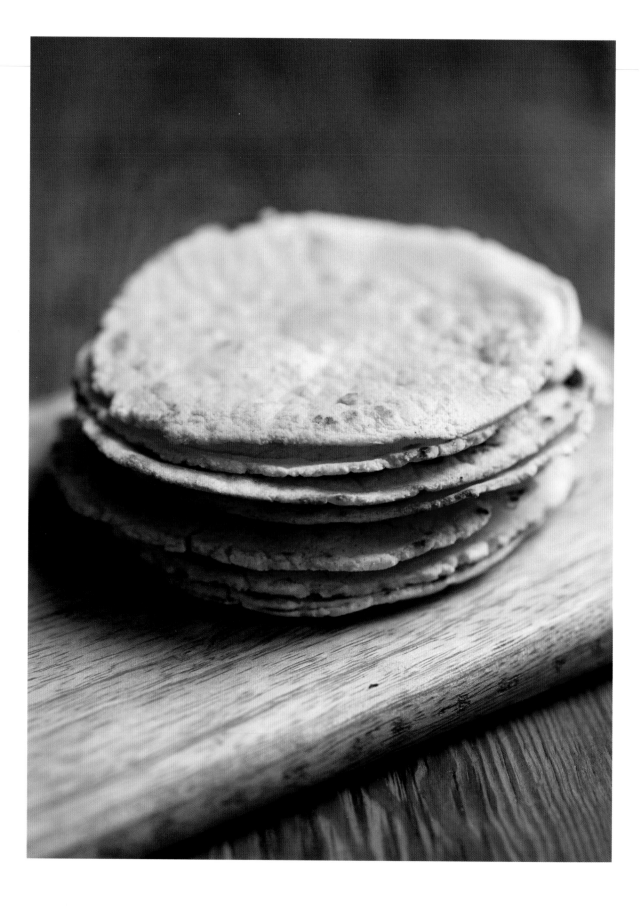

HOMEMADE CORN TORTILLAS

MAKES 8 TORTILLAS

approx. 5 inches in diameter

Prep time: 20 minutes

Resting time: 30 minutes

Cooking time: approx. 3 minutes per tortilla

INGREDIENTS

1¼ cups masa harina flour

¾ cup just boiled water

½ teaspoon sea salt

GF, V+, DF

Corn tortillas are made with masa harina flour (flour made from cooked corn kernels), which you can buy in specialty stores and online. Homemade corn tortillas may not look as perfectly shaped as their store-bought cousins, but I think they have so much more flavor, and using corn flour means these tortillas are gluten-free. Any leftovers can be wrapped up in foil and kept in the freezer until you need them. When it's time to use them, I give them a light sprinkle of water, then wrap them in aluminum foil and heat in the oven.

METHOD

Put the flour into a medium mixing bowl. Gradually stir in the hot water with a wooden spoon. Then use your hands to knead the mixture together to form a ball. Wrap the dough in plastic wrap and leave in the fridge for 30 minutes.

Take the dough out of the fridge and cut it into eight equal pieces. Using your hands, roll each piece into a ball. Now take two sheets of wax paper and sandwich one of the dough balls between them. Using a rolling pin, roll out the dough between the two sheets. Turn the tortilla 90 degrees clockwise then roll again, and keep turning and rolling until the tortilla is very thin, about ⅛ inch. Repeat with the rest of the dough balls.

Place a medium to large, heavy-bottomed frying pan (no oil) over medium-high heat. Once the pan is hot, place the corn tortillas in, two at a time if space allows. Cook them for 1½–2 minutes on one side, pressing down with a spatula if necessary to deflate any air bubbles that may form. Then flip them over with a spatula and cook on the other side for 1½–2 minutes more, until cooked through. Stack the cooked tortillas on a plate as you go and cover with a clean dish towel (the tortillas will steam slightly and become softer and more pliable).

These are now ready to go. I use them for the Tostadas Deluxe (p. 100).

TOSTADAS DELUXE

MAKES 4 TORTILLAS
(1 or 2 tortillas per person)

Prep time: 10 minutes

Cooking time: 5 minutes

INGREDIENTS

2 tablespoons light olive oil or
vegetable oil

1 14-ounce can pinto or black
beans, drained

1 medium clove garlic, finely chopped

½ teaspoon ground cumin

1 small or medium red onion,
finely chopped

1 ripe tomato, finely chopped

1 tablespoon chopped jalapeño

1 avocado, halved, pitted, peeled
and cut into small cubes

1 tablespoon finely chopped
cilantro or parsley

pinch sea salt, or to taste

1 tablespoon freshly squeezed lime
juice (approx. ½ lime)

1 teaspoon extra-virgin olive oil

4 ready-made corn or flour tortillas,
approx. 5 inches in diameter
(store-bought, or see recipe for
Homemade Corn Tortillas on p. 99)

⅔ cup goat cheese or feta, crumbled

GF

Corn tortillas topped with a chunky bean spread and then sprinkled with cheese, red onion, jalapeño, tomato, avocado, and lime. Tostadas are a staple in my home because they're healthy, quick, and easy to make and so satisfying. In a way, they have replaced toast as a base on which to build a great snack or light meal.

METHOD

Preheat the oven to 350°F.

Heat the oil in a medium frying pan, add the beans, and partially mash them with a fork or potato masher. Then add the garlic and ground cumin and fry for 5 minutes.

In a medium bowl, mix together the red onion, tomato, jalapeño, avocado, cilantro, and a small pinch of sea salt. Add the lime juice and extra-virgin olive oil, and toss the ingredients together.

Heat the tortillas by wrapping them in foil and popping them into the warm oven for about 5 minutes.

To assemble the tostadas, spread the bean mixture over the base of each heated tortilla, then spoon the salad mix over the top and finish with a crumbling of cheese.

CORNBREAD WITH JALAPEÑO AND SWEET CORN NIBLETS

MAKES 12 PIECES

Prep time: 15 minutes

Cooking time: 20 minutes

INGREDIENTS

¼ cup cornmeal or fine polenta, plus more for dusting the pan

1 cup all-purpose or spelt flour

2 teaspoons baking powder

½ teaspoon baking soda

⅔ cup milk

1 tablespoon honey

2 large free range eggs

⅔ cup whole milk yogurt

2 tablespoons butter, melted

2 tablespoons jalapeños, chopped

⅓ cup corn niblets, cut fresh from the cob (or frozen and thawed, or canned and drained)

I like a fresh warm batch of this cornbread in a basket to pick at with this Mexican menu, but I also love it served alongside the One-Pot Chili on p. 194. And sometimes I simply have it warm with a little butter spread on top for a great snack.

METHOD

Preheat the oven to 400°F. Grease a 9 x 9-inch baking pan and dust with cornmeal or polenta.

In a large bowl, mix the cornmeal (or polenta) with the plain (or spelt) flour, baking powder, and baking soda.

In a separate bowl, combine the milk, honey, eggs, yogurt, and melted butter. Gradually stir this mixture into the bowl of dry ingredients until thoroughly combined, but do not overmix.

Now stir in the jalapeños and corn niblets. Immediately pour the batter into the baking pan and bake for about 20 minutes until golden brown.

Cut into 12 pieces and serve warm.

MUSHROOM AND CHEESE QUESADILLAS

SERVES 4

Prep time: 5 minutes

Cooking time: 12 minutes

INGREDIENTS

2 tablespoons light olive oil or
    vegetable oil

3½ cups mushrooms, thinly sliced

2 cloves garlic, finely chopped

8 ready-made soft tortillas, approx.
    7¾ inches in diameter (you can
    buy gluten-free)

1¾ cups sharp Cheddar, grated

2 tablespoons finely chopped
    cilantro or parsley

2 tablespoons jalapeños,
    roughly chopped

GF

So quick to make and so addictive, these quesadillas (hot tortilla sandwiches) also make a great lunch, served simply with a crisp green salad tossed in a lemon and olive oil dressing.

METHOD

Heat the oil in a medium frying pan over medium-high heat. Add the mushrooms and fry for 2 minutes, stirring often. Add the garlic and fry for 2 minutes more, until the mushrooms are browned and the juices have evaporated.

Spoon the mushrooms evenly over four of the tortillas, then sprinkle the cheese, herbs, and jalapeños over the mushrooms and sandwich each one with another tortilla on top.

Heat a clean, medium frying pan (no oil) over medium-high heat, then add the first quesadilla and cook for about 1–5 minutes, or until lightly browned and crisp. Carefully flip the quesadilla over, using a spatula, and cook on the other side until it's golden brown and the cheese has gone nice and melty. Remove from the pan and set aside to keep warm.

Repeat with the remaining quesadillas. Once they are all cooked, cut each quesadilla into quarters.

Eat while hot.

MEXICAN-INSPIRED RICE

SERVES 4–6

Prep time: 10 minutes

Cooking time: approx. 25 minutes
(depending on rice cooking time)

INGREDIENTS

1 tablespoon light olive oil or
vegetable oil

1 medium onion, finely chopped

3 cloves garlic, finely chopped

1⅔ cups uncooked brown rice

3⅓ cups hot vegetable stock

4 ripe tomatoes, skinned and finely
chopped (see p. 65 for how to skin
the tomatoes)

1 medium-hot red chili, deseeded
and finely chopped, or ½ teaspoon
chili flakes (optional)

2 tablespoons finely chopped fresh
cilantro or parsley, or 2 teaspoons
dried herbs

1 lime, cut into 4 wedges

GF, V+, DF

This tomato- and onion-infused rice makes a really great side dish that sits happily alongside these Mexican recipes—although I'd gladly eat a bowlful on its own with some grated cheese and chopped parsley sprinkled on top!

METHOD

Heat the oil in a medium, heavy-bottomed saucepan, then add the onion and fry for 2 minutes. Stir in the garlic and the uncooked brown rice and cook through for 1 minute. Pour in the hot vegetable stock and mix in the tomatoes and the chopped red chili (if using).

Cover and simmer gently until the stock has evaporated. This will take around 20-25 minutes (depending on the type of rice you use—check the package for instructions). Test the rice, and add more stock if it's not ready yet.

Once the rice is cooked, turn off the heat, remove the lid, and cover the pan with a clean, dry dish towel. Leave for about 5 minutes. This will absorb the steam and leave the rice fluffy and separated.

Mix in the cilantro or parsley with a fork and serve with a lime wedge on each plate to squeeze over before eating.

AVOCADO, SCALLIONS, AND LIME

SERVES 4

Prep time: 5 minutes

INGREDIENTS

2 ripe avocados (½ per person)
2 scallions, finely chopped
2 limes, halved
pinch sea salt

GF, V+, DF

This is a very simple dish, but the trick to making it really great is to use perfectly ripe avocados. I can't get enough of avocados, and the extra bonus is just how healthy they are for you. They're a rich source of essential healthy fats. I'm always happy when being healthy involves eating more of something I love. It's the perfect accompaniment to Tostadas Deluxe (p. 100) and Mushroom and Cheese Quesadillas (p. 105).

Make sure the rest of your meal is ready to go before you serve this—the avocado will start to go brown if it's left hanging around.

METHOD

Cut the avocados in half lengthways and remove the pits. Using a metal dessertspoon, gently scoop out the flesh, keeping it intact. Slice the scooped-out avocado, sprinkle with the chopped scallions, a squeeze of lime, and a pinch of sea salt. Ready to serve.

MIXED PEPPERS

SERVES 4

Prep time: 5 minutes

Cooking time: 7 minutes

INGREDIENTS

1 red pepper

1 yellow pepper

1 orange or green pepper

1 tablespoon light olive oil
   or vegetable oil

juice of ½ lime

1 teaspoon chipotle paste

pinch sea salt, or to taste

GF, V+, DF

This is a wonderful, brightly colored side dish. With the addition of the chipotle paste, the peppers take on a delicious smoked flavor. Chipotle paste is made from dried, smoked jalapeño peppers. If you don't have any you can use a pinch of chili flakes instead.

METHOD

Remove the woody stem, core, and seeds from the peppers and cut the flesh into ⅓-inch strips.

Heat the oil in a large frying pan over medium-high heat. Add the peppers and toss in the oil for 2 minutes. Add the lime juice and chipotle paste and toss to coat the pepper strips evenly. Continue to cook over medium-high heat for 5 minutes more. Serve either hot or at room temperature.

CUCUMBER AND WATERMELON SALAD

SERVES 4–6
Prep time: 10 minutes

INGREDIENTS
For the dressing:
1 tablespoon extra-virgin olive oil
2 tablespoons lime juice
pinch sea salt

For the salad:
2 cups watermelon
½ cucumber (approx. 1½ cups)
2 tablespoons pumpkin seeds
2 cups arugula (about a handful)

GF, V+, DF

The combination of watermelon and cucumber provides a juicy salad that, to me, symbolizes summer on a plate. It's a great counterbalance to the slightly spicy food in the rest of this menu.

METHOD
Make the dressing first. In a cup or small bowl, whisk together the olive oil, lime juice, and pinch of sea salt, using a fork.

For the salad, peel the watermelon and cut into ¾-inch chunks—remove the seeds if you like. Place in a sieve to allow any juices to drain while you prepare the other ingredients.

Cut the cucumber into four pieces, lengthways, and peel, if desired. Then cut into ¾-inch cubes.

Toast the pumpkin seeds in a dry, heavy-bottomed frying pan for a few minutes until they crisp up, then turn off the heat and transfer to a small dish as soon as they start to color. Be careful not to burn them.

Put the cubes of watermelon and cucumber into a large serving bowl, then drizzle the dressing over them and mix together. Finally, toss in the arugula and toasted pumpkin seeds just before serving.

DAD'S MARGARITA

SERVES 2

Prep time: 10 minutes

INGREDIENTS

1 lime, halved, for rubbing around
    the rim of the glass

finely ground sea salt, for lightly
    salting the rim of the glass

2 shots of tequila

2 shots of Cointreau, or 1 shot
    Cointreau and 1 shot triple sec

juice of 1 orange

juice of 3 limes

ice cubes

GF, V+, DF

This is my dad's recipe, which has been adopted by friends and family everywhere. It has a real kick to it, so please drink it responsibly. I have to say, Dad makes the best margarita I have ever tasted, period!

METHOD

To salt the rims of the glasses, run the half-cut lime around the rim of each glass. Fill a saucer with superfine sea salt. Dab each glass lightly into the salt, turning it slowly so that the outer rim is covered (not the inside or it will make your cocktail too salty when you take a sip).

Mix the remaining ingredients (except the ice) in a cocktail shaker, adding the ice at the last minute, then shake vigorously, pour, and enjoy!

MANGO GRANITA

SERVES 4

Prep time: 10 minutes

Freezing time: 3–6 hours or overnight

INGREDIENTS

3 ripe sweet mangoes, peeled and cut away from the pit

1 teaspoon finely grated lime zest

1 cup water

1 tablespoon freshly squeezed lime juice (approx. ½ lime)

1 passion fruit, halved, for garnish

GF, V+, DF

This refreshing sorbet-like dessert requires the flesh of juicy, ripe mangoes and provides a tangy finish to this Mexican-inspired menu.

METHOD

Chop the mangoes roughly into chunky pieces and put in a food processor with the lime zest. Process until completely smooth—about 1-2 minutes—stopping the machine to scrape down the sides with a rubber spatula as needed. Transfer the purée to a medium bowl and add the water and lime juice. Stir with a large spoon to combine.

Pour the purée into a 8 x 8-inch metal baking pan or any metal pan of a similar size that will fit into your freezer. (This size works best because it provides a large surface area, which helps speed up the freezing process.)

Put the purée into the freezer and stir every 30 minutes, being sure to scrape the ice crystals off the sides and into the middle of the pan, until the mixture is too frozen to stir—this should be about 3 hours, depending on how cold your freezer is. Use a large dinner fork to stir and scrape and break up the ice crystals.

When you're ready to serve the granita, scoop it into chilled glasses or bowls (if it has been in the freezer overnight, you may need to take it out 10 minutes beforehand to allow it to soften slightly). I like to spoon a few passion fruit seeds on top of each serving.

AFTERNOON

TEA PARTY

AFTERNOON TEA PARTY

For 12

The afternoon tea party is a tradition going back years: sipping on tea, snacking on sandwiches and cakes and cookies and chit-chatting the afternoon away. What could possibly be better? You can use any number of excuses—celebrating the arrival of a special guest, a birthday, a baby shower, or just having friends over for a treat. For the food, I like a balance between a selection of savory and sweet treats, freshly prepared sandwiches cut into bite-sized pieces, plates of cookies, and a centerpiece loaf cake that my guests can help themselves to throughout the afternoon.

MENU

Sandwich Selection

Fava Bean Dip - GF, V+, DF

Coconut Loaf Cake

Moist Carrot and Apple Madeleines - DF

White Chocolate Chunk Cookies - GF, DF

Florentines - GF, V+, DF

Peanut Butter Cookies - GF, DF

SANDWICH SELECTION
CHOOSE 2 OR 3 COMBINATIONS PER TEA PARTY

I think I could live on sandwiches! I like to make a variety, both closed and open-faced, and I have suggested a couple options using oatcakes or crackers for a change. You can keep it simple by using just one type of sandwich bread and serve it several different ways, or experiment with a variety of breads, from seeded to gluten-free. Traditionally, you would trim off the crusts of the sandwiches for a tea party—if you choose to do this you can reuse the crusts by pulsing them in a food processor and then storing them as breadcrumbs to cook with at a later date. (Any of these suggestions can be gluten-free if you use gluten-free bread or oatcakes.)

Sliced Boiled Egg with Mayonnaise and Chopped Watercress with a squeeze of fresh lemon juice and a sprinkle of sea salt (see p. 79 for Eggless Mayonnaise recipe) - GF, DF

Smoked Applewood Cheddar with Red Cabbage and Grated Apple Coleslaw (for the coleslaw, grate some red cabbage and apple, then mix with mayonnaise and a squeeze of fresh lemon juice), or smoked applewood Cheddar with sliced peach - GF

Reduced Fat Crème Fraîche, Roasted Red Pimento Pepper, and Chives on an oatcake or buckwheat cracker - GF

Peanut Butter and Raspberry Jam on an oatcake or buckwheat cracker - GF, V+, DF

Chopped Banana with Honey and Cream Cheese - GF

Emmental Cheese, Dijon Mustard, Sliced Cucumber, Pickle, and Sauerkraut - GF

Oven-Roasted Red Onions with Goat Cheese, Chili Jam, and Crisp Lettuce - GF

Hummus and Thinly Sliced Cucumber, or hummus with sliced pickled beetroot (see p. 54 for Hummus recipe) - GF, V+, DF

FAVA BEAN DIP

SERVES 4–6

Prep time: 10 minutes (if using podded broad beans); 20 minutes (if removing the outer skin)

Cooking time: 5 minutes

INGREDIENTS

18 ounces shelled fava beans, or 3 cups frozen fava beans in their skins (most supermarkets or specialty stores sell these), defrosted

2 scallions, thinly sliced

2 teaspoons vegetable bouillon powder

zest and juice of ½ lemon

3 tablespoons extra-virgin olive oil

2 tablespoons mayonnaise

½ tablespoon finely chopped fresh mint

½ tablespoon finely chopped fresh basil

½ teaspoon chili flakes (optional)

GF, V+, DF

Fava beans (broad beans) are a delicious and often overlooked ingredient, and if you want a change from hummus, they make a fabulous, vibrant green dip that's great served with vegetable sticks, on little gem lettuce leaves, or spread onto oatcakes, or other crackers, with thinly sliced radish. For a vegan option, use Eggless Mayonnaise (p. 79).

METHOD

If using frozen fava beans in their skins, place the beans in hot water for 2 minutes, then gently squeeze out the vibrant green beans from their skins.

Place the beans in a medium saucepan with the scallions, bouillon powder, and just enough water to cover the beans.

Bring to a boil and then lower the heat to a gentle simmer. Cook for 2 minutes, then remove from the heat. Do not drain. Reserve a few beans for the garnish, then add all the other ingredients to the pan and blend with a stick blender or in a food processor (or you can just mash with a potato masher).

Add a little extra water if the mix is too thick. Chill the dip and when you are ready to serve, garnish with the reserved beans.

COCONUT LOAF CAKE

SERVES 10–12

Prep time: 20 minutes

Cooking time: 50 minutes

INGREDIENTS

For the sponge:

2¼ cups all-purpose or spelt flour

1½ teaspoons baking powder

1¼ cups desiccated coconut, packed

zest of ½ lemon

1¼ cups sugar

2 large free range eggs

2 teaspoons vanilla extract

⅓ cup butter, melted, plus more
   for greasing the pan

¾ cup coconut milk

For the icing:

1 cup confectioners' sugar, sifted

1½ tablespoons water

For decoration (optional):

1 cup coconut flakes

This loaf cake, flavored with a hint of coconut, brings a little glamour to the table. It's easy to make, fluffy, and delicious. It makes a pretty centerpiece to a tea party with the white icing dripping down the sides.

METHOD

Preheat the oven to 350°F. Grease and line a 9 x 5-inch loaf pan.

Sift the flour and baking powder into a large mixing bowl, then add the desiccated coconut and lemon zest.

In a medium bowl, beat the sugar and eggs together, then stir in the vanilla extract, melted butter, and coconut milk.

Make a well in the center of your flour mixture and then gradually pour in the coconut milk and egg mix, stirring until it's well combined with the dry ingredients. Now pour the batter into the prepared loaf pan.

Bake for 50 minutes, then check by inserting a skewer into the center of the cake. If it comes out clean, the cake is done—if not, put it back in the oven for another 5 minutes and then check again.

Turn the cake out of the pan onto a wire rack or plate and allow it to come to room temperature before icing.

While the cake is cooling, mix the sifted confectioners' sugar with the water in a bowl and beat until smooth. The icing needs to be thick enough to coat the back of a spoon. If it's too thin, add a little more sifted confectioners' sugar; if it's too thick, add a few more drops of water. Remember to do it little by little.

Pour the icing over the cake evenly, making sure you cover the entire surface and letting it drizzle down the sides. While it is still wet, scatter with coconut flakes (if using) and serve.

MOIST CARROT AND APPLE MADELEINES

MAKES 6

Prep time: 15 minutes
Cooking time: 15 minutes

INGREDIENTS

¾ cup all-purpose or spelt flour

½ teaspoon baking powder

¼ teaspoon ground cinnamon

¼ teaspoon baking soda

¼ teaspoon salt

1 medium free range egg,
   lightly beaten

¼ cup soft light brown sugar
   or coconut sugar, packed

⅛ cup vegetable oil, plus more
   for greasing the pan

1 medium carrot (approx.
   ⅔ cup), grated

½ apple, peeled and grated
confectioners' sugar, for sprinkling
   on top (optional)

DF

Madeleines are traditional small cakes from northeastern France. They are baked in a tray of small cake molds shaped like shells. If you don't have a madeleine pan, you can bake them in small cupcake wrappers in a cupcake pan instead (just don't serve the madeleines in the wrappers). The addition of grated carrot and apple gives these cakes extra texture and bite.

METHOD

Preheat the oven to 350°F. Lightly grease a metal or silicone madeleine pan (or use small cupcake wrappers in a cupcake pan).

Sift the flour, baking powder, cinnamon, baking soda, and salt into a medium bowl and stir to combine.

In a separate, larger bowl, whisk together the egg and sugar until fluffy, then stir in the vegetable oil and grated carrot and apple.

Add the dry ingredients to the wet ingredients, stirring until just blended. Spoon the madeleine mixture into the prepared pan and bake for about 15 minutes (or until cooked through—the tops of the madeleines should spring back when touched).

Remove from the oven and let cool slightly in their pan, then gently remove each madeleine from the pan and lay onto a wire rack to cool. Dust with confectioners' sugar just before serving for a pretty finishing touch.

These will keep for 2–3 days in an airtight container.

WHITE CHOCOLATE CHUNK COOKIES

MAKES APPROX. 18 COOKIES
Prep time: 10 minutes
Cooking time: 8 minutes

INGREDIENTS

7 tablespoons butter (or coconut
   oil for dairy-free option),
   plus more for greasing the pans
½ cup coconut sugar
   or granulated sugar
1 large free range egg
1 tablespoon cocoa powder
1¼ cups buckwheat flour
   (for gluten-free option)
   or all-purpose or spelt flour
3½ ounces white chocolate,
   broken into small pieces

GF, DF

I like to make a batch of cookies to keep in a cookie jar, ready to offer to friends when they come over for tea, and I love to see the kids arrive home and head straight for the jar. I usually make these gluten-free, and use coconut sugar and coconut oil, because they are delicious and it makes me feel less guilty when I eat three in a row!

METHOD

Preheat the oven to 350°F and lightly grease two baking sheets.

Cream together the butter (or oil) and sugar in a large bowl until light and creamy. Beat in the egg, cocoa powder, and flour until all the ingredients are well combined. Stir in the white chocolate pieces, making sure they are distributed evenly throughout the mixture.

Drop teaspoonfuls of the cookie dough onto the prepared baking sheets, leaving a 1½-inch space between each cookie to allow room for them to spread during baking. Flatten them slightly with the back of a fork.

Bake for 8 minutes (do not overbake—they will seem a bit underdone but will set nicely on cooling). Use a spatula to ease the cookies off the baking sheets onto a plate and let them cool before eating.

These cookies will keep for up to 5 days in an airtight container.

FLORENTINES

MAKES 20

Prep time: 15 minutes

Cooking time: 10 minutes per batch

INGREDIENTS

vegetable oil, for greasing the trays

4 tablespoons butter (or coconut
butter for dairy-free option)

⅓ cup superfine sugar

2 tablespoons buckwheat flour (for
gluten-free option) or all-purpose
or spelt flour

2 tablespoons half and half (or soy
cream for dairy-free option)

½ cup almonds, roughly chopped,
or flaked almonds

¼ cup shelled pistachios, chopped

zest of 1 lemon

zest of ½ orange

⅓ cup dried cranberries,
roughly chopped

5¼ ounces dark chocolate
(minimum 70% cocoa solids),
broken into chunks

GF, V+, DF

*My second son got me into florentines. They're sweet, nutty, fruity,
zesty—and they have chocolate too! The perfect sweet treat.*

METHOD

Preheat the oven to 350°F. Lightly grease two baking sheets with
vegetable oil. (Alternatively, you can use one baking sheet and
cook the florentines in two batches.)

Warm the butter, sugar, and flour in a small saucepan over a medium
heat, stirring often, until the butter has melted. Remove from the heat,
allow to cool slightly, and gradually add the cream, stirring well until
combined. Add the almonds, pistachios, lemon and orange zest, and
cranberries, and mix well until everything is thoroughly combined.
Drop 1 heaped teaspoonful of the florentine mixture at a time on the
prepared baking sheets, leaving a 1-inch space between each one so
they don't spread into each other during baking. Press them down
a little with the back of the spoon to flatten.

Bake the florentines for 10 minutes, or until golden brown. Remove
from the oven and set aside to cool on baking sheets for a couple
minutes. Then carefully lift them off with a palette knife and transfer
to a wire cooling rack or plate.

Melt the chocolate chunks in a heatproof bowl suspended over a pan
of simmering water (not letting the bowl touch the water). Stir until
smooth and melted.

When the florentines are completely cool, flip them over so that the
flat base is facing upward. Spread the melted chocolate lightly and
evenly over the bases and set aside to cool and set. If you are not
serving these right away, you can store the florentines in layers
between sheets of wax paper in an airtight container for up to 5 days.

PEANUT BUTTER COOKIES

MAKES APPROX. 24 COOKIES

Prep time: 10 minutes

Cooking time: 8–9 minutes

INGREDIENTS

1¼ sticks butter (or 1⅛ cups coconut
  oil for dairy-free option)

½ cup coconut sugar or
  granulated sugar

1 large free range egg

7 tablespoons crunchy peanut butter

1⅛ cups buckwheat flour (for gluten-
  free option) or all-purpose or
  spelt flour

GF, DF

My eldest son first made these cookies for me last summer. As I've been eating less and less gluten recently, he adapted his recipe to make it gluten-free. Once a batch of these cookies is made they do not stick around for long. I now keep a supply of coconut sugar in the pantry because it has a sweet caramel flavor and is a good source of minerals (it's available in specialty stores and most supermarkets).

METHOD

Preheat the oven to 350°F. Line two baking sheets with wax paper.

Cream together the butter (or oil) and sugar in a large bowl until light and creamy. Beat in the egg and crunchy peanut butter. Finally, mix in the flour until all the ingredients are well combined.

Take 1 heaping teaspoon of the mixture at a time and place them on the baking sheets about 1½ inches apart, to allow for any spread during baking. You should have about 24 small balls of cookie dough. Flatten them slightly with the back of a fork.

Bake the cookies for 8–9 minutes until golden brown. Then ease them off the baking sheets and onto a plate to cool. These cookies will keep for up to 5 days in an airtight container.

DINNER

....

FOR TWO

DINNER FOR TWO

There are people in your life that you want to make time for, whether it's a best friend, a family member, or your partner. Taking the time to make a special meal for that someone means you can really concentrate on turning it into an occasion and show how much you care. I always find people are more relaxed, and the conversation flows much better, if it's over good food . . . and wine. Although all of the recipes in this menu are for two, they can very easily be doubled, or tripled, if you're cooking for more.

MENU

Warm Mushroom Salad - GF, V+, DF

Individual White Onion and Tarragon Tarts - GF

Green Beans with Sesame Seeds and Lemon - GF, V+, DF

Individual Chocolate Almond Tortes - GF, DF

WARM MUSHROOM SALAD

SERVES 2

Prep time: 10 minutes

Cooking time: 15 minutes

INGREDIENTS

4 new potatoes, chopped into
   bite-sized cubes

1½ tablespoons light olive oil

3 cups mixed mushrooms
   (e.g. shitake, oyster, chestnut
   mushrooms), sliced

1 clove garlic, finely chopped

1 teaspoon fresh thyme leaves,
   woody stalks removed

1 teaspoon tamari (for gluten-free
   option) or soy sauce

2 teaspoons freshly squeezed
   lemon juice

2¾ cups mixed salad leaves
   (approx. 2 handfuls)

For the dressing:

2 teaspoons extra-virgin olive oil

squeeze of fresh lemon juice
   (1 teaspoon)

sea salt and freshly ground black
   pepper, to taste

GF, V+, DF

This combination of warm sautéed mushrooms tossed in a tangy salad dressing, and then piled on top of new potatoes and fresh dressed salad leaves, is a really satisfying first course. Makes the perfect quick lunch, too.

METHOD

Place the bite-sized new potatoes in a pan of water and bring to a boil. Simmer gently for 10 minutes, or until just tender. Drain, then set aside to cool.

Heat the olive oil in a medium frying pan over medium heat. Add the sliced mushrooms and chopped garlic and sauté for about 5 minutes, or until just beginning to brown. Add the fresh thyme and stir gently. Turn off the heat. Now stir in the tamari or soy sauce and the lemon juice.

When ready to serve, dress the salad leaves. Place the leaves in a medium bowl along with the cooled new potatoes, then drizzle with the olive oil, a squeeze of fresh lemon juice, a sprinkle of sea salt and black pepper, and toss together. Divide between two serving plates and heap the mushrooms on top.

INDIVIDUAL WHITE ONION AND TARRAGON TARTS

SERVES 2

Prep time: 30 minutes
Chilling time: 20 minutes
Cooking time: 35 minutes

INGREDIENTS

For the pastry:

¾ cup all-purpose or spelt flour,
  plus more for dusting the pan
  and worktop
3½ tablespoons salted butter,
  chilled and cut into cubes (keep
  the cubes in the fridge until you
  need them), plus more for
  greasing the pan
1 tablespoon iced water
1 free range egg, beaten, or a little
  milk, for brushing on the pastry

For the filling:

1 tablespoon light olive oil
¾ cup white onions (approx. 2
  medium), halved and thinly sliced
⅓ cup shallots (approx. 3 medium),
  roughly chopped
4 tablespoons white wine
1 tablespoon butter
1 tablespoon all-purpose,
  buckwheat, or spelt flour
⅔ cup milk
1 teaspoon whole-grain mustard
1 tablespoon finely chopped
  fresh tarragon
sea salt and freshly ground black
  pepper, to taste

GF

I love the flavor combination of the onions and shallots encased within this comforting white wine, fresh tarragon, and whole-grain mustard sauce. These indulgent and warming tarts are easy to make, but they look—and taste—so good. You can make the pastry in advance, as it keeps chilled in the fridge for up to 5 days. Just take it out 10 minutes before rolling to allow it to reach room temperature. And of course, if you're short on time, you can use store-bought pastry instead (and you can get gluten-free pastry).

METHOD

First, make the pastry. If using a food processor, put the flour and butter in the processor bowl and pulse until it resembles bread-crumbs. Pour in the chilled water and mix again until the dough just comes together into a ball. Wrap the ball in plastic wrap and chill in the fridge for at least 20 minutes. Take it out 10–15 minutes before you are ready to use it (depending on how warm your kitchen is).

If mixing by hand, make sure you don't let the butter get too warm and overworked; the less you handle it with warm hands the better. Place the flour in a mixing bowl and add the cold cubes of butter. Using your fingertips, gently blend the butter into the flour until you have formed crumbs, leaving some larger pea-sized clumps, too. Add the water and, using a metal spoon, mix to bring the mixture together into a soft ball of dough. Wrap it in plastic wrap and chill in the fridge as above.

To make the individual pastry shells, turn over a metal muffin pan, then grease the underside of two muffin cups with butter and dust with flour (so the pastry won't stick later), leaving at least one cup space between them to allow for easy removal of the pastry shells when cooked. Lightly dust a clean worktop with flour. Cut the dough into two equal portions and roll each one into a ball shape. Gently roll out the first pastry ball, turning it 45 degrees each time you roll to ensure the pastry doesn't split. Continue to roll and turn until the pastry is about ⅛-inch thick. Repeat with the second portion of pastry.

Gently lift the pastry circles and place over the greased upturned muffin pan, then carefully shape them to fit the upturned cups. Trim away any excess pastry with scissors or a sharp knife. Place the pan in the fridge to chill for 10 minutes—this will keep the pastry shells from shrinking as they bake. Preheat the oven to 400°F.

Brush the outside of the pastry shells with the egg or milk and place on the middle rack of the oven for 10–12 minutes, or until they start to turn a light golden color. Remove from the oven and allow to cool for a few minutes, then carefully ease the pastry shells off the cups of the pan and place them, bottom-down, on a baking sheet—the right way up now! Put them back in the oven for 5–7 minutes more until lightly crisp, then remove and set to one side while you make the filling.

Turn the oven down to 350°F. To make the filling, warm the olive oil in a small frying pan over medium heat. Add the onions and shallots and sauté gently for 2 minutes. Pour in the wine and allow to sizzle in the pan, stirring occasionally, for 8–10 minutes, until the onions have softened and are just starting to turn brown.

In the meantime, melt the butter in a small saucepan over low heat, mix in the flour, and heat through until you have formed a paste. Take off the heat and mix in the milk a little at a time, using a whisk in order to keep the sauce from getting lumpy. Place back over medium heat and stir often with a whisk for 2–4 minutes until you have a smooth, thick sauce.

Stir in the mustard, chopped tarragon, and the onion mixture, then season with a pinch of sea salt and grind of black pepper to taste. Scoop the mixture generously into the two pastry shells.

Pop the tarts back into the oven for 8–9 minutes, until they are cooked all the way through.

GREEN BEANS WITH SESAME SEEDS AND LEMON

SERVES 2

Prep time: 5 minutes

Cooking time: 5 minutes

INGREDIENTS

1¾ cups green beans, trimmed

1 teaspoon sesame seeds

1½ teaspoons butter, or
    1 teaspoon extra-virgin olive oil

squeeze of fresh lemon juice
    (approx. 1 teaspoon)

sea salt and freshly ground black
    pepper, to taste

GF, V+, DF

A very simple side dish that is crisp, flavorful, and super-healthy. Green beans are a great source of protein, vitamins K, A, and C, as well as manganese and dietary fiber.

METHOD

Bring a medium saucepan of water to a boil. Place the beans in a colander or steamer above the water, cover with a lid, and steam until tender—about 3-5 minutes.

Meanwhile, heat a small or medium frying pan over medium heat and toast the sesame seeds until lightly golden (this should only take a minute or two). Quickly transfer them to a saucer to prevent burning.

Now, in the same frying pan, heat the butter or olive oil over low heat, add the green beans and sesame seeds, and squeeze a little lemon juice over them.

Transfer the cooked beans to a serving bowl and season with salt and freshly ground pepper. Serve immediately with Individual White Onion and Tarragon Tarts (p. 148).

These beans work just as well served at room temperature, as a salad.

INDIVIDUAL CHOCOLATE ALMOND TORTES

SERVES 2

Prep time: 15 minutes

Cooking time: 12 minutes

INGREDIENTS

7 tablespoons salted butter or coconut oil, plus more for greasing the ramekins

cocoa powder, for dusting the ramekins

3½ ounces dark chocolate (minimum 70% cocoa solids), broken into even-sized chunks

2 large free range eggs, separated

½ cup ground almonds or pistachios (can be ground in food processor)

¼ cup superfine sugar

2 ramekins

GF, DF

The pairing of bitter dark chocolate with smooth ground almonds is seductive. When you bite into the center of a torte, you get a soft, melting, and delicious mouthful. By using ground almonds instead of flour, you have a gluten-free dessert that is easy to make, but never fails to impress. The tortes can be kept unbaked in the fridge for 1–2 days, or frozen for up to 3 months. If frozen, allow 30 minutes to defrost before baking.

METHOD

Preheat the oven to 350°F. Grease two ramekins with butter and dust with cocoa powder. Melt the butter and dark chocolate together by warming the butter in a small pan over very low heat and then adding the chocolate chunks, stirring often, until the chocolate has just dissolved. Make sure the melting chocolate doesn't cook for too long; if it overheats it will become grainy instead of smooth. Take off the heat and transfer the chocolate sauce to a medium mixing bowl. Allow it to cool slightly for about 5 minutes.

Mix the egg yolks into the cooled chocolate mixture. Add the ground almonds and sugar and beat together. Then, in a separate, clean bowl, whisk the egg whites with a clean whisk until they form soft peaks. Gently fold the whisked egg whites into the chocolate mix.

Divide the chocolate mixture evenly between the ramekins and bake for 12 minutes, until the tops are just springy to the touch. You want the centers to be gooey, so be careful not to overcook them. Wearing oven mitts to protect your hands, remove the ramekins from the oven and gently tip them upside down to pop the tortes out onto a serving dish.

You can eat these tortes as they are, but I love them with a few fresh raspberries or strawberries and a spoonful of vanilla ice cream or whipped cream.

KIDS'

MENU

KIDS' MENU

Let's face it: Cooking for kids can be fairly ungratifying at times. You put all that thought and energy into making them nutritious meals just so you can get comments like, "How many bites do I have to have?" The kids know when I'm trying to get "healthy" food into them and just shut up shop.

To make life easier, and in the hope of some enthusiastic feedback, I've designed some simple, one-stop-shop meals for my kids, and their friends, that I know they like, and then I can sneak in some of the things that are good for them, too. They're happy—and so am I. Phew!

MENU

Alphabet Soup - GF, V+, DF

Super Mac 'n' Cheese - GF

All-in-One Burrito - GF, V+, DF

Fruit Chunks and Chocolate Dippy Sauce - GF

Let Them Have It Fruit Popsicles - GF, V+, DF

ALPHABET SOUP

SERVES 6

Prep time: 15 minutes
Cooking time: 30 minutes

INGREDIENTS

2 tablespoons light olive oil or
    vegetable oil
1 medium onion, finely chopped
1 stick celery, finely chopped
1 carrot, finely chopped
¾ cup green beans, trimmed and
    finely chopped, or broccoli florets,
    finely chopped
1 14-ounce can chopped tomatoes
1 teaspoon mixed dried herbs
1 14-ounce can cannellini beans,
drained
3 cups vegetable stock
1 bay leaf
½ cup mini alphabet-shaped pasta
    (or gluten-free small pasta)

GF, V+, DF

By using tiny alphabet-shaped pasta, I can produce a soup that my kids find entertaining as well as tasty. The letters make it fun to eat, and it has a great assortment of vegetables and small white beans for protein and extra texture. I often serve this with toast spread with hummus for them to dunk in. If you can't find tiny alphabet pasta, you can use small macaroni instead, or spaghetti broken up into small pieces.

METHOD

Heat the oil in a medium to large saucepan over medium heat, then add the chopped onion, celery, carrot, and green beans (or broccoli). Gently sauté for 5 minutes, before stirring in the chopped tomatoes, and mixed herbs.

Bring to a boil and then reduce the heat and simmer gently for 10 minutes. Now stir in the cannellini beans, vegetable stock, and bay leaf. Bring the soup back to a simmer, cover, and cook for 15 minutes more.

Meanwhile, in a separate, small saucepan, cook the pasta, following the instructions on the package, and drain.

Stir the cooked pasta into the soup. Remember to fish out the bay leaf just before you serve the soup.

SUPER MAC 'N' CHEESE

SERVES 4–6 (4 for older kids and
6 for younger ones)

Prep time: 15 minutes
Cooking time: 20–25 minutes

INGREDIENTS

2 cups macaroni (or rice and
  corn pasta macaroni for
  gluten-free option)

½ head cauliflower (approx. 9
  ounces), broken into small florets

2 tablespoons light olive oil or
  vegetable oil or butter

3 tablespoons buckwheat flour (for
  gluten-free option) or all-purpose
  or spelt flour

2⅛ cups milk

1 teaspoon Dijon mustard

1¾ cups sharp Cheddar, grated

¾ cup frozen peas

freshly ground black pepper,
  to taste (optional)

2 tablespoons grated Parmesan
  cheese, or similar

GF

This is a classic mac 'n' cheese, with small cauliflower florets and peas (both powerhouses of nutrition) mixed in. The kids love it and I am happy because they get two extra vegetables snuck in.

METHOD

Preheat the oven to 350°F. You will need a 8 x 8 inch ovenproof dish (or similar-sized dish) for this recipe.

Fill a medium saucepan with water, bring the water to a boil, and add the pasta. Cook until just cooked through (al dente), according to the instructions on the package. Drain, rinse under cold water, and set aside.

Take the small cauliflower florets and steam over a steamer for about 7 minutes, or until just cooked through. Alternatively place florets in a medium saucepan of boiling water for about 6 minutes.

Drain the cauliflower in a sieve and run under cold water to stop it from cooking. Set aside while you make the cheese sauce.

To make the cheese sauce, gently heat the oil (or butter) in a medium to large saucepan, then mix in the flour and stir with a wooden spoon until it forms a soft paste. Remove from the heat and gradually stir in the milk, using a wooden spoon or hand whisk, to prevent lumps from forming.

Put the sauce back onto the heat and bring to a gentle bubble, stirring continuously until the sauce thickens, about 2–3 minutes. Turn off the heat and stir in the mustard and Cheddar. Now add the frozen peas, and then gently mix in the cooked pasta and cauliflower. Add a little pepper if desired (you may not need salt as the cheese is quite salty). Spoon the mixture evenly into the ovenproof dish.

Sprinkle with the Parmesan cheese and bake for 15 minutes, or until the sauce bubbles and is golden brown on top.

ALL-IN-ONE BURRITO

SERVES 6

Prep time: 15 minutes
Cooking time: 20–25 minutes

INGREDIENTS

1 cup brown rice

2 tablespoons light olive oil or
vegetable oil

1 medium onion, finely chopped

1 clove garlic, finely chopped

1 14-ounce can kidney beans,
drained

1 14-ounce can chopped tomatoes

1 teaspoon agave syrup or honey

½ cup green beans, trimmed and
chopped small

⅓ cup corn kernels, cut fresh from
the cob (or frozen and defrosted,
or tinned and drained)

2 teaspoons dried mixed herbs or
1 tablespoon chopped fresh parsley

6 ready-made soft corn or
flour tortillas

¾ cup Cheddar (or non-dairy
cheese), grated

GF, V+, DF

The trick here is not to overstuff the tortillas, as they need to be tightly wrapped around the filling so that your kids can eat them with their hands. They are fun to eat and packed with healthy ingredients: a great source of fiber and protein, while the kidney beans provide iron, too.

METHOD

Cook the rice in a pot of boiling water, following the instructions on the package. I usually do one part rice to two parts boiling water, then cover with a lid and simmer for 20–25 minutes until the rice is cooked. Do not stir it while it is cooking. Test a bite and, if it is not quite ready, add a little more water. Then turn off the heat, remove the lid, and cover the pan with a clean dish towel to absorb the steam so you don't end up with wet rice.

While the rice is cooking you can start the tomato sauce. Heat the oil in a medium–large frying pan over medium-high heat. Sauté the onion for 7 minutes, then stir in the garlic and drained kidney beans. Cook for a couple minutes, then stir in the canned tomatoes and agave syrup or honey. Simmer gently for 10 minutes, then stir in the green beans, corn, and mixed herbs. Simmer for 10 minutes more.

When the rice is ready, mix into the tomato sauce. Preheat the oven to 325°F.

Wrap the tortillas in foil and warm them in the oven for 5 minutes. Carefully remove the foil and put the tortillas on plates. Put a couple spoonfuls of the rice and tomato mix onto the middle of each tortilla, followed by a sprinkle of grated cheese, making sure that you don't overfill them, as you need to leave room to wrap the tortillas tightly around the filling. Taking one tortilla at a time, fold the bottom of the tortilla up toward the center, then fold in one side at a time to form a tortilla wrap. Now pick it up and take a bite!

FRUIT CHUNKS AND CHOCOLATE DIPPY SAUCE

SERVES 4

Prep time: 10 minutes
Cooking time: 5 minutes

INGREDIENTS

For the chocolate sauce:

3½ ounces milk chocolate
   (I like Green & Black's)
6 tablespoons milk

Fruit of your choice, such as:

2 kiwi fruits, peeled and quartered
1 banana, peeled and sliced
   into chunks
8 strawberries, hulled and cut in half
1 ripe mango, peeled and cut into
   bite-sized cubes
blueberries
pineapple chunks

GF

Easy to make, bright, colorful—and it's a joy to watch children eating this.

METHOD

Break the chocolate into pieces and place in a small saucepan along with the milk. Put the pan over low heat and keep stirring until all the chocolate has just melted and you have a glossy sauce, then take off the heat. Be careful not to overheat the chocolate or it will burn and take on a gritty texture.

Prepare a selection of your child's favorite fruit. You can either thread the fruit onto wooden skewers or put it into a bowl and use forks.

Pour the chocolate sauce into one bowl to share, or into eggcups for individual portions (my kids love doing it this way). Ready to eat!

LET THEM HAVE IT
FRUIT POPSICLES

MAKES 8 POPSICLES
(of four different flavors)
Prep time: 15 minutes
Freezing time: Overnight

INGREDIENTS

8 strawberries, plus 3 tablespoons
    apple juice
12 raspberries, plus 2 tablespoons
    apple juice
1 ripe mango and 1 banana,
    plus 3 tablespoons orange juice
1 ripe banana and 1 ripe peach,
    plus 3 tablespoons apple juice

Popsicle molds or small paper cups
8 lollipop sticks or teaspoons

GF, V+, DF

I get the kids involved in making these. That way, they can have input in the flavor combinations they like best and we can experiment. These Popsicles are a perfect summery treat, and kids of all ages love making them—including me. Each fruit combination below makes two popsicles, or you can quadruple the quantities in your favorite fruit combination to make eight of the same flavor.

METHOD

Prepare the fruit: hull the strawberries; peel the mango, and remove the pit, then chop into chunks; peel and chop the banana; remove the pit from the peach and chop into chunks.

Blend each of your chosen fruit and juice combinations in a blender, or with a stick blender in a pitcher, until smooth. Pour into Popsicle molds or small paper cups, insert a stick or teaspoon into each one, so it stands upright, and freeze overnight or until frozen through.

BE PREPARED

DINNER PARTY

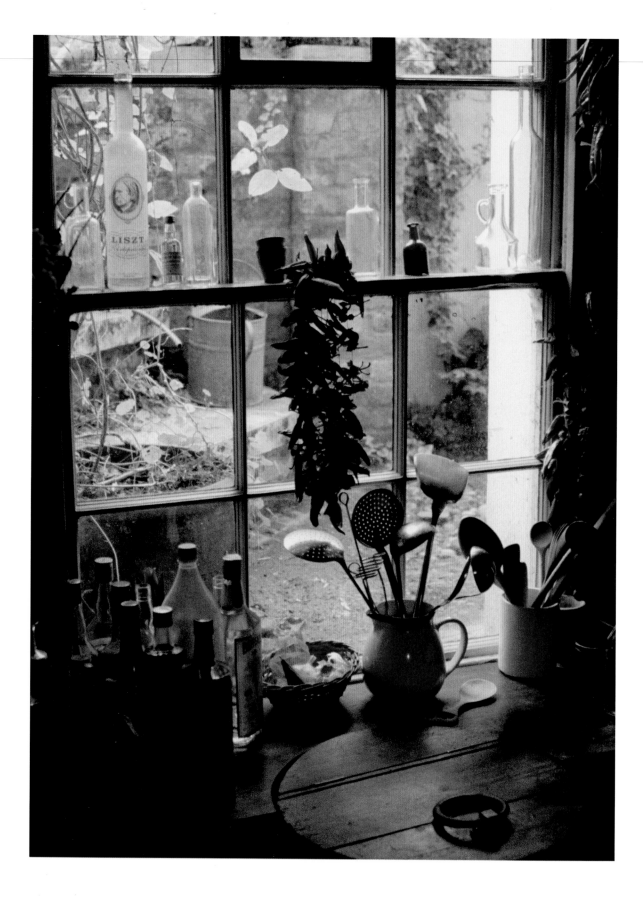

BE PREPARED DINNER PARTY

I enjoy having friends over for dinner and a catch-up. I want to cook something that will impress them but still be able to enjoy myself and not be so busy in the kitchen that I miss out on the latest laughs and news. So this menu is designed around recipes that you can prepare in advance, and then just heat up or finish off easily when your guests arrive.

MENU

Super Pea and Watercress Soup with Grilled Cheese Croutons - GF, V+, DF

Zucchini and Leek Fritters with Feta Citrus Dressing - GF

Herb and Cheese Soufflé - GF

Wilted Spinach - GF, V+, DF

Baked Plums with Fresh Basil and Amaretti Crisp - GF, V+, DF

SUPER PEA AND WATERCRESS SOUP
WITH GRILLED CHEESE CROUTONS

SERVES 6

Prep time: 10 minutes
Cooking time: 25 minutes

INGREDIENTS

For the soup:

2 tablespoons light olive oil or
   vegetable oil
2 medium white onions,
   roughly chopped
2 cloves garlic, roughly chopped
1 medium potato, roughly chopped
1 teaspoon dried mixed herbs
4¼ cups vegetable stock
3 cups peas (fresh or frozen)
2 cups watercress, washed
pinch sea salt and freshly ground
   black pepper, to taste

For the cheese croutons:

2 slices whole-wheat sandwich bread,
   or other sliced bread of your choice
butter (or non-dairy alternative) for
   spreading on the bread
1 cup grated or sliced sharp Cheddar
   or goat Cheddar (or non-dairy
   cheese slice)

GF, V+, DF

This is a gorgeous, vibrant green soup. The peas add a subtle sweetness and the watercress a fresh peppery, mustardy taste. Watercress is my favorite leaf and I try to eat it every day. It's a superfood packed with nutrients such as vitamins A, C, and K, and is a good source of iron and antioxidants. The little grilled cheese croutons sprinkled on top of this soup add the perfect finishing touch. This dish is ideal as a dinner-party first course—you can make the soup the day before and keep it in the fridge, then all you have to do is prepare the croutons just before you serve the soup. It's great for lunch, too.

METHOD

Heat the oil in a large saucepan over medium heat and sauté the onions, garlic, and potato for 4 minutes. Stir in the mixed herbs and vegetable stock, bring to a boil, then turn down the heat and simmer gently for 10 minutes. Add the peas to the pan, bring back up to a gentle simmer, and cook for 10 minutes more, then turn off the heat.

Stir in the watercress, then blend with a stick blender to create a vibrant green, smooth soup. (Or you can let it cool slightly and then pour all the ingredients into a blender or food processor before blending.) Add a pinch of sea salt and black pepper to taste.

To make the croutons, heat a medium frying pan and butter one side of each slice of bread. Place one slice, butter-side down, into the frying pan and cover with the grated cheese.

Then place the second slice of bread, butter-side up, on top of the cheesy bread in the frying pan. Cook until golden brown on the underside, then flip the sandwich over to cook the other side. It needs about 2 minutes on each side, until the outside of the sandwich is crisp and golden and the cheese has melted. Turn off the heat and transfer the sandwich to a chopping board. Using a sharp knife, cut the sandwich into small cubes to form croutons. Sprinkle a few croutons on top of each bowl of soup before serving.

ZUCCHINI AND LEEK FRITTERS
WITH FETA CITRUS DRESSING

MAKES 12 FRITTERS (2 per person), approx. 3 inches in diameter
Prep time: 15 minutes
Cooking time: 10–12 minutes

INGREDIENTS
9 ounces zucchini (about
   2 medium), trimmed
9 ounces leeks (1 medium), trimmed
   and finely chopped
1 red onion, finely chopped
1 tablespoon finely chopped fresh
   dill, or 1 teaspoon dried dill
1 tablespoon finely chopped fresh
   parsley, or 1 teaspoon dried parsley
zest of 1 lemon
1 tablespoon nutritional yeast flakes
   or tamari (for gluten-free option)
   or soy sauce
¾ cup buckwheat flour (for gluten-
   free option) or all-purpose
   or spelt flour
3 free range eggs, beaten
sea salt and freshly ground black
   pepper, to taste
light olive oil or vegetable oil
   (approx. 4 tablespoons), for frying

For the dressing:
¾ cup feta cheese, crumbled
3 tablespoons plain yogurt
3 tablespoons freshly squeezed
   lemon juice (approx. 1½ lemons)

GF

Zucchini and leeks go so well together. These fritters have a good hit of lemon zest and fresh herbs so they are bursting with flavor. The feta citrus dressing is brilliantly tangy and great for dipping or drizzling on top.

METHOD
Preheat the oven to 325°F. Grate the raw zucchini and lay it evenly on a clean dish towel or paper towel, then roll up to soak away the excess juice. Set aside until ready to use.

To make the dressing, put the feta, yogurt, and lemon juice into a blender and blend for about 10 seconds. Transfer to a serving bowl or pitcher and set to one side. If you do not have a blender, mash the ingredients together with a fork.

In a medium mixing bowl, combine the chopped leeks, red onion, dill, parsley, lemon zest, and nutritional yeast flakes (or tamari or soy sauce). Stir in the flour and then the beaten egg. Finally stir in the grated zucchini and season with a pinch of sea salt and freshly ground black pepper. Make sure all the ingredients are well mixed together.

Heat the oil over medium-high heat in a large frying pan. There should be sufficient oil to just cover the base of the pan. When the oil is hot, take 1 teaspoonful of the leek and zucchini fritter mixture and spoon into the pan, then flatten the fritter with the back of the spoon so it is about 3 inches wide. Continue with another 2 or 3 spoonfuls of mixture at a time, ensuring there is enough space in between to be able to turn your fritters.

Cook for about 2 minutes on each side, or until golden and cooked through. Drain on paper towels, then wrap in foil and keep warm in the oven while you make the rest of the fritters. Once you've cooked them all, serve them immediately, either with the dressing alongside in a small bowl for dipping, or drizzled over the top.

HERB AND CHEESE SOUFFLÉ

SERVES 4–6
Prep time: 30 minutes
Cooking time: 35–40 minutes

INGREDIENTS

2¾ tablespoons butter, plus more for
  greasing the dish
½ cup buckwheat flour (for gluten-
  free option) or all-purpose or
  spelt flour
1⅔ cups milk, at room temperature
1 teaspoon English or Dijon mustard
6 large free range eggs, separated
2 cups sharp Cheddar or
  Gruyère, diced
¾ cup Parmesan, grated
2 tablespoons of a combination of
  three of the following fresh herbs,
  finely chopped: sage, thyme,
  oregano, marjoram, parsley
freshly ground black pepper, to taste

GF

Mum would often ask me to make her a cheese soufflé, so I grew up loving making them. The common perception is that soufflés are difficult to get right, but as long as you cook them properly they're pretty straightforward. For a dinner party, I make one large soufflé—a main-course showstopper—instead of individual ones. I prepare the cheese sauce ahead of time and then whisk the egg whites and stir them into the sauce just before I'm ready to put it in the oven.

METHOD

Preheat the oven to 400°F. Butter a 6-inch soufflé dish or a similar-sized ovenproof dish.

You can prepare the cheese sauce in advance, if you want to. To make the sauce, melt the butter in a medium pan over medium heat. Stir in the flour, using a wooden spoon, until a firm paste is formed. Remove from the heat and add the milk a little at a time, stirring continuously with a hand whisk until there are no lumps. Place back on the heat and keep stirring until the sauce has thickened—about 4-5 minutes. Remove from the heat and allow to cool slightly before stirring in the mustard, egg yolks, cheeses, herbs, and a little black pepper to taste. (You probably won't need salt as the cheese is already quite salty.) Transfer the sauce to a large mixing bowl.

To finish the soufflé, whisk the egg whites in a separate, clean bowl, using an electric whisk, until they form stiff peaks. Stir 2 heaping tablespoonfuls of the whisked egg whites into the cheese sauce to loosen and lighten it. Then gently fold in the rest of the whisked whites with a large metal spoon; a light touch is important so that you don't bash out the bubbles.

Gently pour this mixture into the prepared soufflé dish. Bake on the middle rack of the oven for 35-40 minutes (35 minutes if you like a slightly runny center or 40 minutes for a firmer center), until well risen and brown on top. This soufflé goes particularly well with Wilted Spinach (p. 183).

WILTED SPINACH

SERVES 6

Prep time: 1–2 minutes

Cooking time: 1 minute

INGREDIENTS

1 bunch spinach, washed well

1 teaspoon extra-virgin olive oil
   or melted butter

squeeze of fresh lemon juice

small pinch sea salt

freshly ground black pepper, to taste

GF, V+, DF

A very simple side dish—and so nutritious. This is my favorite way to eat spinach, and it forms a good counterbalance to the richness of Herb and Cheese Soufflé (p. 181). You can start cooking this when the soufflé is almost ready.

METHOD

Put the spinach into a medium-large pot, cover, and cook over medium heat for 1-2 minutes, until all the leaves have just wilted. Drain well in a colander. While the spinach is draining, heat the olive oil or melted butter in the pot. Then add the wilted spinach, lemon juice, and salt, and stir together. Season with black pepper and it's ready.

BAKED PLUMS WITH FRESH BASIL AND AMARETTI CRISP

SERVES 6
Prep time: 7 minutes
Cooking time: 20 minutes

INGREDIENTS

12 ripe plums (approx. 18 ounces)
8 tablespoons maple syrup
8 fresh basil leaves, thinly sliced
12 amaretti cookies, crushed

GF, V+, DF

This dessert is perfect for a last-minute dinner party because it's quick and easy to make. You can have everything prepared in advance and then just put the plums in the oven when you're ready to bake. Despite its simplicity, this is an impressive dessert that packs a real flavor punch—and is so pretty and aromatic, too. (If you need this to be gluten-free, check that your amaretti biscuits are made with almonds and have no added flour.)

METHOD

Preheat the oven to 325°F. Cut the plums in half and remove the pits. Lay the plum halves, cut-side up, evenly on a medium baking sheet. Drizzle with the maple syrup, then bake for 20 minutes until soft and juicy.

Remove from the oven and scatter the basil leaves over the baked plums, then sprinkle with the crushed amaretti cookies. Transfer the plums to a serving dish.

I think this pudding is delicious served with a spoon of crème fraîche, vanilla ice cream, or soya cream.

BONFIRE

PARTY

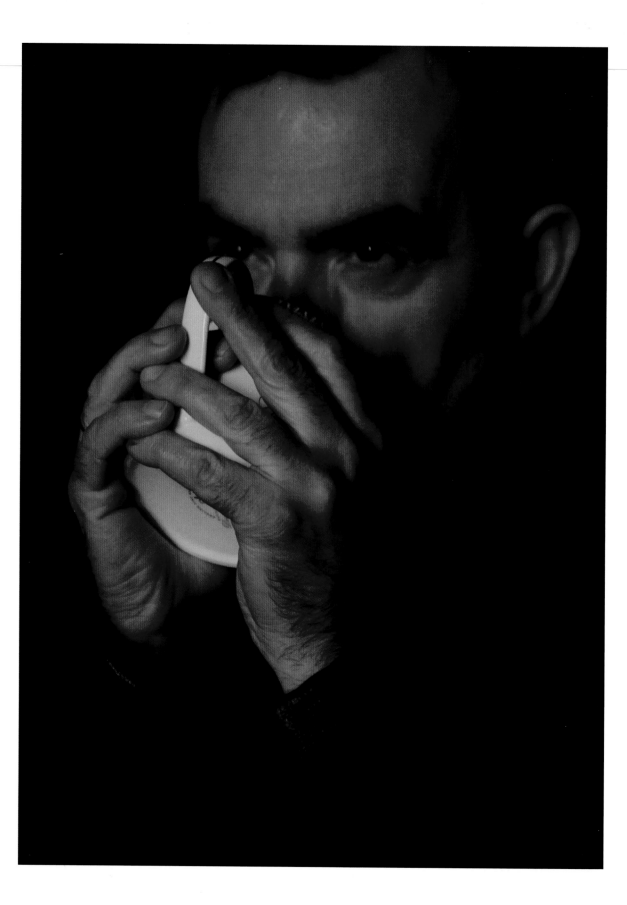

BONFIRE PARTY

My family loves a bonfire. I have fond memories of my dad putting out bales of hay around the fire and we would sit together, warming ourselves by the flames, eating and telling stories. So when I thought about this menu, my head was full of crisp autumn evenings warmed by the glow of the bonfire flames. These are family-friendly, warming recipes to be enjoyed outside.

MENU

Incredibly Onion Soup with Garlic Toasts - GF, V+, DF

One-Pot Chili with Baked Potatoes - GF, V+, DF

Apple Wedges with Caramel Dipping Sauce - GF, V+, DF

Ginger and Pine Nut Cookies - GF, DF

Luxury Hot Chocolate - GF, V+, DF

INCREDIBLY ONION SOUP
WITH GARLIC TOASTS

SERVES 6

Prep time: 15 minutes

Cooking time: 1 hour

INGREDIENTS

For the soup:

3 tablespoons light olive oil or
   vegetable oil

6 medium white onions (approx.
   5¼ cups), thinly sliced

1 medium leek (approx. 2¾ cups),
   trimmed and finely chopped

3 cloves garlic, finely chopped

1 teaspoon agave syrup or sugar

2 tablespoons buckwheat flour (for
   gluten-free option) or all-purpose
   or spelt flour

2⅛ cups white wine

2 teaspoons dried thyme

1 teaspoon mustard, preferably Dijon

2 bay leaves

4¼ cups vegetable stock

For the garlic toasts:

1 baguette, or 6 slices gluten-free
   bread (allow 1 slice per serving)

3 tablespoons extra-virgin olive oil
   or melted butter

2 cloves garlic, crushed

1 tablespoon finely chopped
   fresh parsley

pinch sea salt

GF, V+, DF

Made with slow-cooked onions and topped with luscious garlic croutons, this soup is perfect for a cold autumn night.

METHOD

To make the soup, heat the oil in a large saucepan over medium heat. Stir in the sliced onions, then turn down the heat to low, cover, and cook gently for 10 minutes, stirring occasionally. Add the leek and the garlic and cook for 5 minutes more.

Take the lid off, then add the syrup or sugar and allow it to cook very gently for 30 more minutes, stirring often. You don't want the onions to get crisp, just golden brown and nicely caramelized.

Now stir in the flour, coating the onions, and heat through for 1 minute. Gradually stir in the white wine, thyme, mustard, and bay leaves and bring to a gentle boil. Then slowly pour in the vegetable stock and simmer gently for 30 minutes.

To make the garlic toasts, cut the bread into ¾-inch-thick slices. In a small bowl, mix the oil or butter with the crushed garlic, chopped parsley, and a pinch of sea salt.

Under the broiler, toast the slices of bread on one side, then turn them over and spread the garlic mixture onto the other side. Put the slices back under the broiler, garlicky side up, for a few minutes until toasted.

Ladle or spoon the onion soup into bowls. Lay the garlic toasts on top of the hot onion soup and serve immediately.

ONE-POT CHILI
WITH BAKED POTATOES

SERVES 6

Prep time: 15 minutes

Cooking time: 40–60 minutes

INGREDIENTS

6 baking potatoes

For the chili sauce:

2 tablespoons light olive oil or
vegetable oil

2 medium onions, finely chopped

2 cloves garlic, finely chopped

1¾ cups green beans, trimmed
and chopped

1 red pepper, deseeded and
finely chopped

1 14-ounce can kidney beans,
drained

12 ounces vegetarian ground beef
substitute (optional)

1 teaspoon chipotle chili paste,
or ½ teaspoon dried chili flakes

2 14-ounce cans chopped tomatoes

4 tablespoons water

1 tablespoon Worcestershire sauce
(vegetarian, no anchovies)

1 tablespoon tamari (for gluten-free
option) or soy sauce

1 tablespoon finely chopped fresh
cilantro or parsley, or 1 teaspoon
dried herbs

sea salt and freshly ground black
pepper, to taste

sour cream or crème fraîche (or
dairy-free plain yogurt), to serve

GF, V+, DF

Juicy, tangy, with a bit of chili heat, and easy to make—this is a one-pot recipe, so you won't have much washing up! I like to use chipotle chili paste, because it's made with smoked jalapeños, and adds a wonderful smoky flavor to the dish.

METHOD

Preheat the oven to 350°F. Wash the potatoes and prick them with a fork. Wrap them in foil and bake in the oven—this should take about 1 hour, depending on the size of your potatoes.

Meanwhile, make the chili sauce. Heat the oil in a medium to large saucepan, add the onions, and fry gently for 5 minutes. Stir in the garlic, green beans, and red pepper. Turn up the heat slightly, then stir in the drained kidney beans and the ground beef substitute (if using) and cook through for 1 minute.

Stir in the chipotle paste or chili flakes, the chopped tomatoes, water, Worcestershire sauce, and tamari or soy sauce. Bring to a gentle simmer, then cover and cook for 30 minutes, checking and stirring occasionally.

Taste, and add more seasoning as necessary. If you prefer a spicier sauce, add extra chipotle paste or chili flakes. The sauce should be rich and thick. Finally, stir in the herbs and add sea salt and black pepper to taste. Keep warm until the potatoes are ready.

To serve, spoon the chili sauce evenly over the baked potatoes and top each one with a dollop of sour cream or crème fraîche.

APPLE WEDGES
WITH CARAMEL DIPPING SAUCE

SERVES 6

Prep time: 5 minutes

Cooking time: 10 minutes

INGREDIENTS

For the caramel dipping sauce:

¾ cup agave syrup

1⅔ cups half and half (or soy cream for dairy-free option)

½ teaspoon ground cinnamon

For the apple wedges:

4 apples

24 wooden skewers

GF, V+, DF

For me, the flavors of apples and caramel conjure up images of autumn get–togethers. As children, we loved it when Mum and Dad got us bobbing for apples—brilliant bonfire party fun!

METHOD

To make the caramel dipping sauce, heat the agave syrup in a medium, heavy-bottomed saucepan. Bring it to a gentle boil and then simmer for about 4 minutes. Be careful not to let it boil too vigorously, as you don't want it to burn. Letting it boil gently will allow the sauce to thicken slightly when it cools.

Meanwhile, in a separate, small saucepan gently heat the cream and cinnamon together; it needs to be warm, since cold cream could curdle when mixed with the hot agave syrup.

When the agave syrup is ready, stir in the warm cinnamon and cream, and simmer for another minute. Take off the heat. At this point, you can use a hand whisk to combine the ingredients well. Pour the caramel sauce into a serving bowl.

Cut the apples into six wedges and cut away any core. Stick wooden skewers into the tops of the apples. Now they're ready to dip into the sauce.

GINGER AND PINE NUT COOKIES

MAKES 24 COOKIES

Prep time: 20 minutes

Cooking time: 7–8 minutes per batch

INGREDIENTS

5½ tablespoons butter (or coconut oil for dairy-free option)

½ cup soft light brown sugar or coconut sugar

1 free range egg, beaten

⅛ cup molasses

1½ cups buckwheat flour (for gluten-free option) or all-purpose or spelt flour

¾ teaspoon baking powder

2 tablespoons ground ginger

1 teaspoon ground cinnamon

¼ teaspoon sea salt

½ cup pine nuts

confectioners' sugar, for dusting the cookies (optional)

GF, DF

These cookies deliver a gingery warming kick—ideal on a chilly night—and the pine nuts give them extra creamy texture.

METHOD:

Preheat the oven to 350°F and line two large baking sheets with baking parchment (or lightly grease them).

In a large mixing bowl or food processor, beat the butter and sugar together until creamy. Mix in the beaten egg and molasses. Gradually sift in the flour, baking powder, ground ginger, cinnamon, and salt, then add the pine nuts. Mix together until all the ingredients are well combined and a stiff dough is formed.

Using 1 heaping teaspoonful of dough per cookie, roll the mixture into balls and place on the baking sheets, leaving a 1-inch space between each cookie, then flatten them slightly with the back of the spoon. Bake for 7–8 minutes, or until just cooked through and slightly crisp at the edges, but still soft on top.

Transfer the cookies to a wire rack to cool. If you like, you can dust with confectioners' sugar before serving.

LUXURY HOT CHOCOLATE

SERVES 6

Prep time: 5 minutes

Cooking time: 5 minutes

INGREDIENTS

3 tablespoons good-quality
   cocoa powder

4½ tablespoons light agave syrup

1½ tablespoons vanilla extract

6⅓ cups milk (or almond, soy, or
   rice milk for dairy-free option)

GF, V+, DF

Chocolate makes me happy. I make a large batch of this chocolate milk, and what isn't used on the night, I pour back into the milk container and keep chilled in the fridge, so I can drink it throughout the week as cold chocolate milk.

METHOD

Mix the cocoa powder and agave syrup together in a bowl or mug, using a fork to make a smooth paste with no lumps. Stir in the vanilla extract. To thin out the chocolate paste, stir in 3 tablespoons of the milk and mix with the fork until well combined.

Now transfer the chocolate paste into a large saucepan. Using a wooden spoon, gradually stir in the remaining milk. Place over medium heat until it is warmed through and just starting to come to a boil. Pour into mugs and enjoy.

KEEPING OUT

THE COLD

KEEPING OUT THE COLD

For 6

I grew up in the countryside and I still try to spend as much time there as possible. This is the type of meal I love to cook after I come in from a brisk horse ride in the winter, and I have several hungry, cold people to feed. For me, it is all about soulful comfort food that leaves you feeling satisfied and warm on those winter evenings. Here, I have drawn on the earthy tastes and flavors of autumn and winter's seasonal ingredients.

MENU

Chili Pumpkin Soup - GF, V+, DF

Mushroom and Chestnut Pie - GF, V+, DF

Red and Green Cabbage Twist - GF, V+, DF

Buttery Carrots with Fresh Herbs - GF, V+, DF

Spiced Poached Pears - GF, V+, DF

Crème Anglaise - GF

CHILI PUMPKIN SOUP

SERVES 6

Prep time: 15 minutes

Cooking time: 30 minutes

INGREDIENTS

2 tablespoons light olive oil or
  vegetable oil

2 medium white onions,
  roughly chopped

2 cloves garlic, chopped

1 carrot, chopped

1 stick celery, chopped

2¼ pounds pumpkin or butternut
  squash, peeled, deseeded, and
  cubed 1 inch

6 fresh sage leaves, or 1 teaspoon
  dried sage

1 medium red chili, deseeded, and
  chopped (or 2 if you like a little extra
  heat), or ½ teaspoon chili flakes

1 medium sweet potato, peeled
  and chopped

1 14-ounce can butter beans (lima
  beans), drained

6 cups vegetable stock

sea salt and freshly ground black
  pepper, to taste

pumpkin seeds, to garnish

drizzle of chili oil or extra-virgin
  olive oil (optional)

spoonful of crème fraîche or soya
  cream (optional)

GF, V+, DF

My mum loved pumpkins; she and Dad grew them every year. So we would carve them for Halloween, but we also cooked many pumpkin recipes throughout the season. I love the combination of pumpkin with a hint of chili heat. Use more or less chili, depending on how hot you like it.

METHOD

Heat the oil in a large, heavy-bottomed saucepan over medium heat, then add the onions, garlic, carrot, and celery and sauté for a couple minutes. Next, add the chopped pumpkin, sage, chili, sweet potato, and butter beans (lima beans), and continue to cook for 2 more minutes.

Add the vegetable stock, stir, and bring to a boil, then turn down the heat to a gentle simmer. Cover with a lid and cook for 25 minutes, or until all the vegetables and beans have softened and cooked through.

Allow to cool slightly before puréeing with a stick blender in the pan. (If using a food processor, let the soup cool slightly, then ladle in small amounts and purée a bit at a time.) After blending, taste and season with sea salt and black pepper if necessary.

Toast the pumpkin seeds in a small, dry frying pan, over medium heat, until they are crisp—about 3 minutes. Don't let them burn. Take off the heat.

To serve, sprinkle a few toasted pumpkin seeds on top of each bowl of soup and drizzle with a little oil and thinly sliced red chili, if desired, or a little crème fraîche.

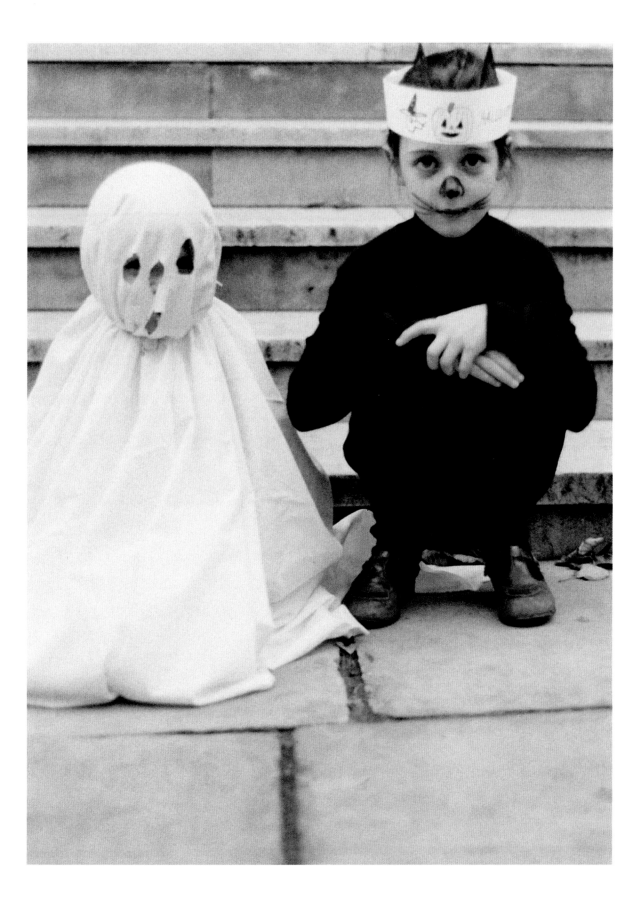

MUSHROOM AND CHESTNUT PIE

SERVES 6

Prep time: 20 minutes
Cooking time: 1 hour

INGREDIENTS

For the filling:

2 tablespoons light olive oil or
vegetable oil

2 medium leeks (approx.
10½ ounces), finely chopped

1 medium red onion, finely chopped

4¼ cups chestnut mushrooms or
similar, thinly sliced

1⅔ cups cooked and peeled
chestnuts, quartered

2 tablespoons tamari or soy sauce

1 tablespoon vegetarian
Worcestershire sauce

1 tablespoon finely chopped fresh
sage, or 1 teaspoon dried sage

1 tablespoon finely chopped fresh
thyme, or 1 teaspoon dried thyme

2 tablespoons finely chopped fresh
rosemary, or 1 tablespoon
dried rosemary

1 tablespoon cornstarch

1½ tablespoons vegetable
stock powder (bouillon)

1⅔ cups cold water

1½ teaspoons (smooth, not grainy)
mustard, preferably English (such
as Coleman's) or Dijon

freshly ground black pepper, to taste

For the pastry:

11¼ ounces ready-made puff pastry
(you can find gluten-free)

flour, for rolling

a little milk or beaten free range egg
(or almond milk), for brushing on top

GF, V+, DF

This is a wonderful traditional pie made with one large piece of puff pastry folded around a mushroom and chestnut gravy filling—easy to make and a great centerpiece to this meal. You can assemble the pie an hour ahead, then brush with milk or beaten egg just before baking.

METHOD

Preheat the oven to 400°F. You will need a 9-inch round pie dish for this recipe.

To make the filling, gently heat the oil in a large, deep-sided frying pan or medium saucepan. Add the leeks, onion, mushrooms, chestnuts, tamari or soy sauce, and Worcestershire sauce. Sauté for about 12 minutes over medium-high heat, stirring often. Add the herbs and cook for 2–3 minutes more, then turn the heat down slightly.

Meanwhile, make the vegetable stock by adding the cornstarch and vegetable stock powder (bouillon) to a mixing bowl, then stirring in the cold water and mixing well. (Don't use hot water or the stock will get lumpy.)

Gradually pour the vegetable stock into the leek and mushroom mixture, stirring gently with a wooden spoon until the mixture reaches a gentle simmer. Add the mustard and cook, stirring often, for 8 or more minutes. It should thicken into a glossy sauce. Season with black pepper to taste and set aside to come to room temperature, about 15 minutes.

Unroll the puff pastry on a clean, lightly floured surface. Gently roll out the pastry a little more until it is about ⅛ inch thick—there needs to be a larger surface area of dough to hang over the edges of the pastry dish—you will need this for when you come to fold it over the filling to close the top of the pie. Loosely line the inside of the pie dish with the pastry, leaving the extra pastry hanging over the edges (a quiche pan with a detachable base works well, if you want to transfer the pie to a serving dish when cooked).

When the mushroom and chestnut filling has cooled, spoon it onto the pastry base and gently spread it evenly around. Now fold the edges of the excess pastry into the center, over the filling, to close the pie. Lightly pinch the edges together so it stays closed. Brush the top of the pie with milk or beaten egg and bake for 35 minutes (allow an extra 5–10 minutes if baking straight from the fridge), until the top of the pie is golden brown.

RED AND GREEN CABBAGE TWIST

SERVES 6

Prep time: 10 minutes

Cooking time: 10 minutes

INGREDIENTS

1 tablespoon light olive oil or
vegetable oil

½ red onion, halved and thinly sliced

2 garlic cloves, finely chopped

1–2 teaspoons caraway seeds,
to taste

3⅛ cups green cabbage
(approx. ½ cabbage), such as
Savoy, shredded

3⅛ cups red cabbage (approx.
⅓ cabbage), shredded

pinch sea salt and freshly ground
black pepper, to taste

zest of 1 lemon

GF, V+, DF

The mixture of green and red cabbage makes for a fabulously colorful side dish that complements the earthy colors of the mushroom and chestnut pie so well. Cabbage doesn't have a good culinary reputation, but cooked properly, it's delicious—and also one of the healthiest vegetables you can eat.

METHOD

Heat the oil in a large frying pan over medium heat. Add the onion and garlic, and turn the heat down to low—this will prevent the garlic and onions from burning—then cook for 3-4 minutes until softened.

Add the caraway seeds and green and red cabbage and turn the heat back up to medium so you can hear a nice sizzle. Cook, mixing often, for 5-7 minutes until the cabbage is lightly cooked, but still a little crunchy. Season with a pinch of sea salt and black pepper to taste. Turn off the heat. Mix in the lemon zest, and it's ready to serve.

BUTTERY CARROTS
WITH FRESH HERBS

SERVES 6

Prep time: 7 minutes

Cooking time: 11 minutes

INGREDIENTS

1⅛ pounds carrots, cut into
  1½-inch strips

6 tablespoons butter or olive oil

pinch sea salt

½ cup water (or enough to nearly
  cover the carrots in the pan)

squeeze of lemon juice

1 tablespoon finely chopped fresh
  herbs, such as tarragon, parsley,
  thyme, or marjoram

GF, V+, DF

A nutritious side dish that adds wonderful color to the meal. Adding butter to the cooking water gives the carrots a lovely glossy glaze, which makes them look and taste special.

METHOD

Lay the carrot strips in a layer in a large frying pan or saucepan, one that has a lid. Add the butter (or oil), a pinch of salt, and the water. Bring to a boil, cover, and cook for about 7 minutes, or until the carrots are tender. Make sure the pan does not completely dry out; you may need to add a little more water from time to time.

When the carrots are just cooked, remove the lid and reduce the cooking liquid until thick enough to glaze the carrots—this should take around 4 minutes. Turn off the heat and drain off any excess liquid. Squeeze a little lemon juice over the carrots, followed by a scattering of fresh herbs. Mix together well, and serve.

SPICED POACHED PEARS

SERVES 6
Prep time: 15 minutes,
Cooking time: 45 minutes
Cooling time: 2 hours

INGREDIENTS

1 bottle (750ml) red wine
(preferably Burgundy)

1⅔ cups water

1 stick cinnamon

1 vanilla pod, split lengthways with
seeds scraped out, or 1 tablespoon
vanilla extract

pared zest of 1 unwaxed lemon
(use a potato peeler)

pared zest of 1 unwaxed orange
(use a potato peeler)

4 whole cloves

3 tablespoons agave syrup

6 firm ripe pears

To serve (optional):
Crème Anglaise (p. 221)

GF, V+, DF

The seasonal spice in this simple dessert delivers a spectacular taste sensation. There are many varieties of pear, and for this recipe you want to choose one that will remain firm when poached. The cooking time will vary, depending on the firmness of your pears, so after about 10 minutes of poaching it's best to test them every few minutes; if you overcook them they will fall apart, and undercooked they will be too crisp. Test by sticking in a skewer to make sure the pear is just tender all the way through. This is great served with the Crème Anglaise (p. 221)—or natural coconut milk yogurt for a dairy-free option.

METHOD

In a large saucepan (big enough to hold all of the pears), place all of the ingredients (except for the pears). Bring to a boil, and then reduce the heat and gently simmer for 10 minutes.

Meanwhile, slice the bottom off the pears slightly, to allow them to sit upright on a flat surface without tipping over. Then, using a melon baller, small knife, or teaspoon, gently scoop the core out from the bottom of the pear. Finally, peel the pears, leaving the stems on.

Gently place the pears upright in the simmering liquid and poach for 10-15 minutes, depending on the firmness of the pears (test them after 10 minutes). Turn off the heat and let them cool in the liquid for 2 hours. This will soften the pears further and allow them to soak up all the flavors of the liquid.

After the pears have finished cooling to room temperature and soaking in the liquid, gently remove them and arrange on serving plates or in bowls. Serve with Crème Anglaise, if desired.

Note: You can remove and discard all the flavorings (cinnamon stick, and peel and cloves) from the poaching liquid and keep the liquid (which can be chilled or frozen) for poaching more pears at a later date.

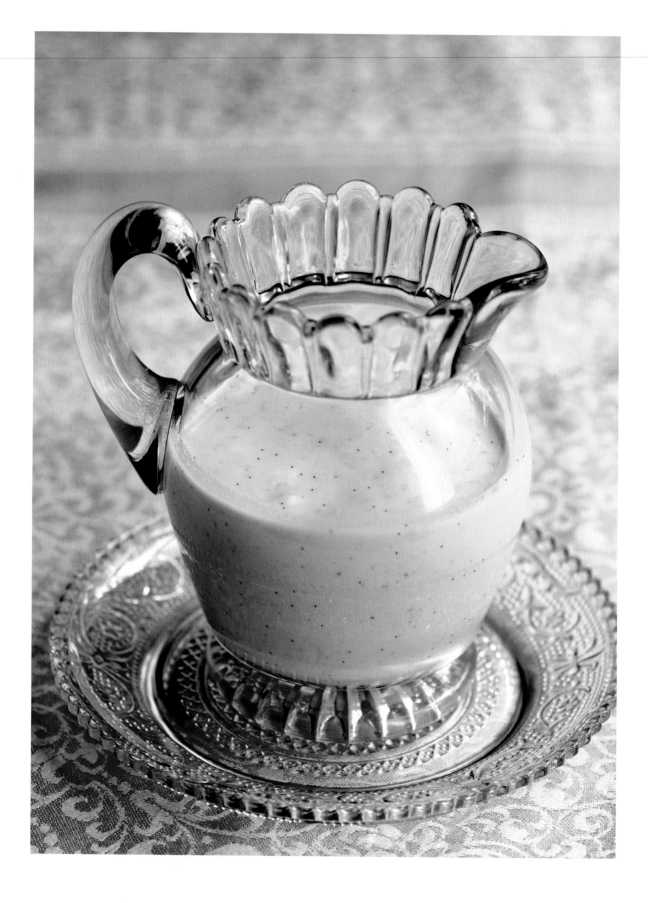

CRÈME ANGLAISE

SERVES 6

Prep time: 12 minutes

Cooking time: 10 minutes

INGREDIENTS

1 ⅔ cups heavy cream

1 vanilla pod, split lengthways,
or 1 tablespoon vanilla extract

5 large free range egg yolks

⅓ cup sugar

GF

This luxuriously creamy vanilla sauce, which I cannot resist, is the perfect match for Spiced Poached Pears (p. 218). I guess you could just call it custard, but I think the French name sounds a bit more exotic!

METHOD

In a medium saucepan, gently heat the cream and vanilla pod (or extract) until bubbles just begin to form around the edges of the pan, then turn off the heat and allow the infused cream to cool slightly. Remove the vanilla pod if using (being careful not to burn your fingers) and scrape out the seeds with either a butter knife or a metal teaspoon. Put the vanilla seeds back into the cream and discard the pod.

Beat the egg yolks and sugar together in a medium mixing bowl until light and frothy. Using a hand whisk, mix a couple tablespoons of the cooled cream and vanilla mixture into the egg yolks, before gradually whisking in the rest. Pour the mixture back into the saucepan over low to medium heat. Stir gently with a wooden spoon until the mixture thickens enough to coat the back of the spoon. To serve, strain through a sieve into a pitcher, to give a smoother consistency.

Note: If the mixture starts to curdle, add a little extra cream and beat gently with a hand whisk until the texture has evened out.

This is also amazing poured over fruit pies or steamed puddings.

FESTIVE

FEAST

FESTIVE FEAST

Where my dad grew up, the Sunday roast was a weekly tradition and a big family occasion. And when we were growing up as vegetarians, my mum and dad were keen to continue the custom of having the family gather around the table for a Sunday feast, vegetarian-style, so we never felt we were missing out. I've borne this in mind when planning this festive menu, which is special enough for the Big Day: a mouthwatering veggie roast with all the trimmings—stuffing, roast vegetables, mashed potatoes, a luscious red wine gravy, a side of vegetables, and an indulgent chocolate dessert.

MENU

Festive Roast - GF, DF

Celebration Stuffing - GF, V+, DF

Roasted Root Vegetables with Rosemary - GF, V+, DF

Baked Broccoli and Cauliflower Florets - GF, V+, DF

Hot Brussels Sprout Coleslaw - GF, V+, DF

Mashed Potatoes Topped with Caramelized Leeks - GF

Red Wine Gravy - GF, V+, DF

Chocolate and Cherry Roulade

FESTIVE ROAST

SERVES 6–8

Prep time: 30 minutes

Cooking time: 45 minutes

INGREDIENTS

⅓ cup raw cashew nuts, chopped small

⅓ cup raw almonds, chopped small

⅓ cup sunflower seeds, roughly chopped

2 tablespoons tamari (for gluten-free option) or soy sauce

2 tablespoons light olive oil or vegetable oil, plus more for greasing the pan

2 medium onions, finely chopped

1 stick celery, finely chopped

2 cloves garlic, finely chopped

¾ cup canned chopped tomatoes

1 carrot, grated

⅔ cup cooked puy lentils (or canned adzuki beans, drained)

1 tablespoon chopped fresh thyme, or 1 teaspoon dried thyme

1 tablespoon chopped fresh rosemary, or 1 teaspoon dried rosemary

1 tablespoon chopped fresh sage, or 1 teaspoon dried sage

1⅛ cups cooked white quinoa

3 tablespoons nutritional yeast flakes

2 tablespoons buckwheat flour (for gluten-free option) or all-purpose or spelt flour

⅓ cup dried cranberries (optional)

2 large free range eggs, beaten

freshly ground black pepper, to taste

GF, DF

I've worked on this recipe over the years and feel it makes a tasty centerpiece for a roast dinner. You can prepare the veggie roast mix the day before and keep it chilled in the fridge. It goes well with roast vegetables, and all the traditional trimmings, with a generous pouring of gravy over the top. I suggest you have a dollop of horseradish sauce on the side, too. This recipe serves six to eight, so double the quantities and cook in two loaf pans if you are making it for a larger gathering. I like to have some left over so I can use it in a sandwich the next day with some Thousand Island Dressing (p. 79) and crisp lettuce leaves.

METHOD

Preheat the oven to 350°F. Grease and line a 9 x 5 inch loaf pan with parchment paper, then brush a little oil on the paper too.

In a dry, heavy-bottomed frying pan over medium heat, toast the chopped cashews, almonds, and sunflower seeds for 2-3 minutes until lightly browned. Add the tamari or soy sauce and toss to coat the nuts. Remove from the heat and transfer the toasted nuts and seeds to a large mixing bowl. Set aside and let cool.

In the same frying pan, heat the oil and gently fry the onions and celery for 10 minutes until golden and cooked through. Add the garlic, chopped tomatoes, grated carrot, and cooked lentils (or adzuki beans), mix well, and sauté for a couple minutes, then transfer to the bowl containing the toasted nuts and mix together. Add the herbs and the remaining ingredients to the bowl and mix until well combined. Season with black pepper to taste.

When you are ready to cook, transfer the mixture to the prepared loaf pan and bake for 30 minutes. Remove from the oven and turn out onto a baking sheet. Peel off the parchment paper, then put the roast back into the oven for 15 minutes more, until golden and cooked through. Let it rest for 5 minutes before slicing—this will allow it to firm up slightly and make it easier to slice. Place on a serving dish and cut into slices with a sharp carving or bread knife.

CELEBRATION STUFFING

SERVES 6–8
Prep time: 20 minutes
Cooking time: 45 minutes

INGREDIENTS

3 slices sandwich bread (approx. 4¼ ounces), cut into 1-inch cubes

7 tablespoons butter, or 4 tablespoons light olive oil or vegetable oil, plus more for greasing baking sheets/dish

2 onions, finely chopped

1 leek, trimmed and finely chopped

2 sticks celery, finely chopped

1 pear, cored and chopped into ⅓-inch pieces

1 tablespoon finely chopped fresh rosemary

2 tablespoons finely chopped fresh sage

1 tablespoon finely chopped fresh parsley

¾ cup pine nuts

freshly ground black pepper, to taste

sea salt, to taste (optional; you may not need extra salt if your stock is already salty)

1 cup vegetable stock

1 large free range egg, beaten (optional)

GF, V+, DF

My mum taught me how to make stuffing. The basics are bread, celery, onions, and herbs. You can make it into balls to bake, or as one whole piece in a baking dish. Gluten-free bread will work here too, as long as it is a light loaf, not too heavy, and if you want a vegan option you can leave out the beaten egg. No festive roast is complete without stuffing, and this recipe fits the bill perfectly. You can prepare it in advance and simply reheat it in the oven when needed.

METHOD

Preheat the oven to 350°F. If making balls of stuffing, lightly grease two baking sheets; if baking in one piece, grease a 9 x 9 inch baking dish.

Spread the cubes of bread on a baking sheet and bake for 10 minutes until crisp. Meanwhile, in a large, heavy-bottomed pan, melt the butter or heat the oil over medium to low heat. Add the onions, leek, celery, and pear and sauté for about 15 minutes until softened and golden.

Mix in the toasted bread cubes, herbs, and pine nuts, and season with black pepper and sea salt to taste. Stir in the vegetable stock and the beaten egg, if using, and leave for 10 minutes to thoroughly soak in.

If making stuffing balls, scoop up 1 tablespoon of stuffing at a time, then mold it into a ball and place on the prepared baking sheet. Or, if baking in one piece, simply press the stuffing mix gently into the prepared baking dish.

Bake the stuffing for 25-30 minutes (25 minutes for balls and 30 minutes if baking in one piece) until crisp and golden on the outside, but still soft on the inside.

ROASTED ROOT VEGETABLES
WITH ROSEMARY

SERVES 6

Prep time: 10 minutes
Cooking time: 65 minutes

INGREDIENTS

18 ounces carrots (approx.
  6 medium), halved

18 ounces parsnips (approx.
  6 medium), trimmed and halved

12 new potatoes or small potatoes,
  halved (or 4 small turnips, trimmed
  and halved)

3 medium sweet potatoes, quartered

2 red onions, quartered

1 head garlic, halved

4 rosemary sprigs

3 tablespoons light olive oil
  or vegetable oil

2 pinches sea salt and freshly ground
  black pepper, to taste

GF, V+, DF

A fantastic combination of root vegetables is an essential part of any festive meal. I heap them all together on a serving dish and let my guests serve themselves. The vegetables can be prepared and parboiled, then set aside, until you're ready to pop them into the oven to roast.

METHOD

Preheat the oven to 350°F. Put the carrots, parsnips, small potatoes (or turnips), and sweet potatoes into a large pot of cold salted water. Bring to a boil, then turn the heat down to medium. Cook for 5 minutes and then drain in a colander. If you are preparing ahead of time, you can now keep in the refrigerator until you are ready to roast the vegetables.

Lay the parboiled vegetables, along with the onions, garlic, and rosemary, on a large baking sheet or divide between two baking sheets. The vegetables will crisp up better if the tray isn't overcrowded. Drizzle with the oil, add a sprinkle of sea salt, and toss together so that the vegetables are lightly coated in the oil.

About 15 minutes before you start to cook the festive roast, pop the vegetables in the oven and roast for 1 hour, making sure to toss after 30 minutes and, if using two baking sheets, switching their position in the oven. Serve the roasted vegetables immediately, seasoned with a little black pepper, if desired.

BAKED BROCCOLI AND CAULIFLOWER FLORETS

SERVES 6
Prep time: 5 minutes
Cooking time: 40 minutes

INGREDIENTS
1 large head broccoli (approx.
    12 ounces)
½ medium to large head cauliflower
1 tablespoon olive oil
½ teaspoon sea salt
squeeze of lemon, to serve

GF, V+, DF

A very easy side dish—I like to roast the broccoli and cauliflower, because it means I can just chuck it in the oven for 40 minutes before we eat. No fuss, but full of flavor and full of goodness, too. If you make a little too much, any leftovers can be turned into a great salad the next day. Simply sprinkle with toasted flaked almonds or pumpkin seeds, then drizzle with a little olive oil, a squeeze of lemon juice, and a pinch of sea salt.

METHOD
Preheat the oven to 350°F and get out a medium to large baking dish.

Break the broccoli and cauliflower into florets, rinse them with cold water, and leave them slightly damp, since this will help the vegetables steam and cook, once they're in the oven. Lay them in your baking dish, drizzle with the olive oil, and sprinkle with sea salt. Toss to ensure all the florets are lightly coated.

Cover the baking dish with foil and bake the vegetables in the oven for 20 minutes. Remove the foil, stir, and cook for 20 minutes more to allow them to brown slightly.

I love these with a squeeze of lemon juice.

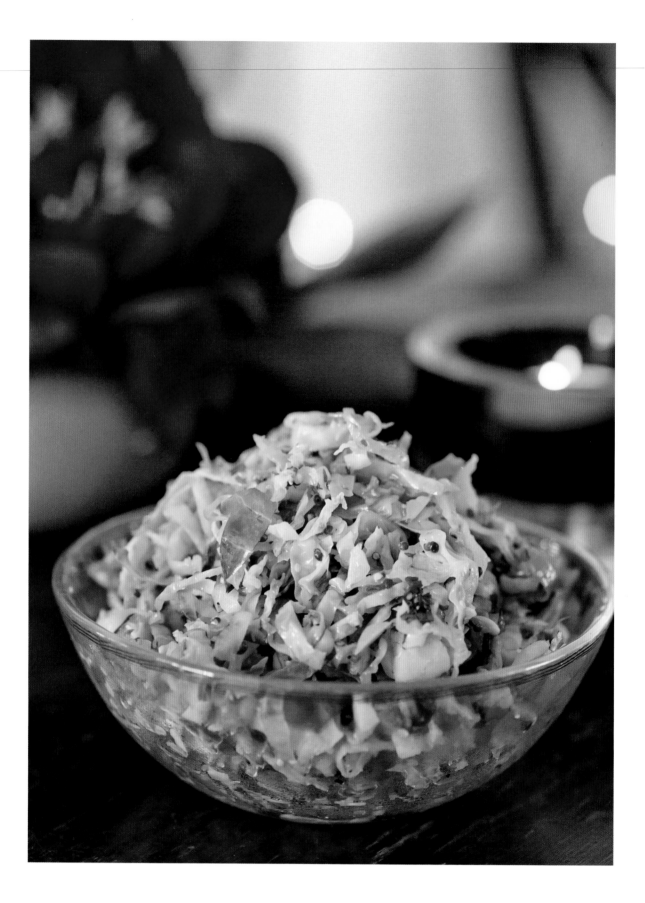

HOT BRUSSELS SPROUT COLESLAW

SERVES 4–6

Prep time: 10 minutes

Cooking time: 3 minutes

INGREDIENTS

1 tablespoon whole-grain mustard

2 tablespoons white wine vinegar

1 tablespoon honey (or
agave syrup)

2 tablespoons extra-virgin olive oil

4½ cups Brussels sprouts, trimmed
and thinly sliced (14 ounces)

1 tablespoon chopped fresh parsley

sea salt and freshly ground black
pepper, to taste

GF, V+, DF

This is the one and only way I like to eat Brussels sprouts. I've never been fond of them, but with this recipe I polish them off, no problem. They are stir-fried to retain their crispness and then tossed in a mustard, honey, and white wine vinegar dressing. Now, I actually have to admit I like them! You can trim and slice the Brussels sprouts and make the dressing ahead of time, then set them aside until you're ready to stir-fry.

METHOD

In a large bowl, whisk together the mustard, white wine vinegar, and honey.

Heat a large frying pan until hot, add the oil, and toss in the Brussels sprouts. Cook for 2 minutes, shaking the pan, until the sprouts are just starting to color. Add the dressing and cook for one more minute. Turn off the heat then toss in the parsley and season with salt and pepper. Transfer to a warmed dish and serve immediately.

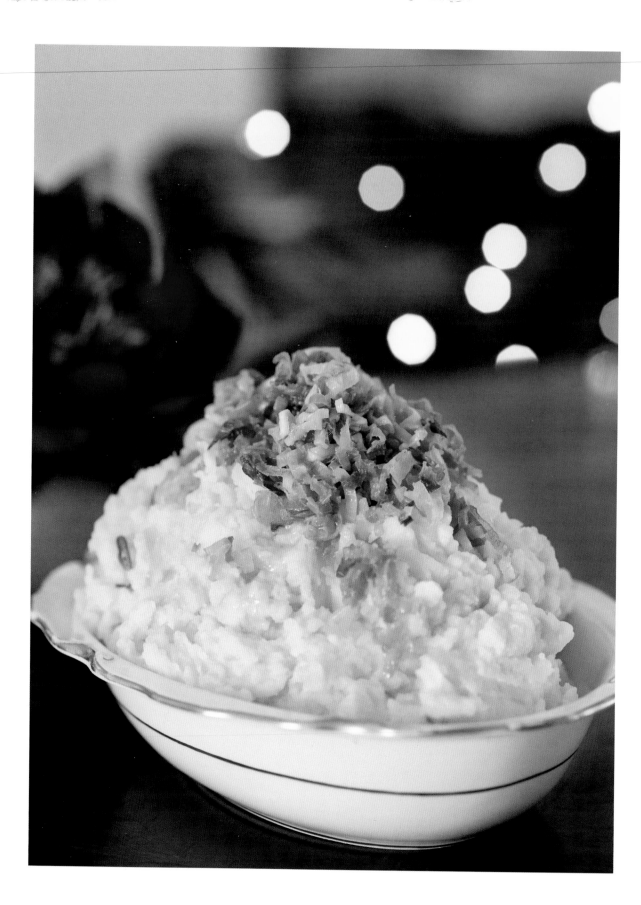

MASHED POTATOES
TOPPED WITH CARAMELIZED LEEKS

SERVES 6
Prep time: 10 minutes
Cooking time: 25 minutes

INGREDIENTS
6 medium potatoes
1 tablespoon light olive oil or
    vegetable oil
1 large leek, trimmed and thinly sliced
sea salt, to taste
¾ cup milk
½ cup butter
1 tablespoon horseradish
    sauce (optional)
freshly ground black
    pepper, to taste

GF

Luxurious mashed potatoes are a classic. They're finished off here with gorgeous, slow-cooked leeks. I sometimes like to stir in a dollop of horseradish sauce for a little extra kick. Any leftovers can been rolled into patty shapes and fried until golden brown, then served with a poached egg on top.

METHOD
Peel and chop the potatoes into 1-inch cubes. Place in a large pot of cold, water, bring to a boil, and then turn down to a gentle simmer for 20 minutes or until cooked through. Drain in a colander.

Meanwhile, to prepare the leeks, heat the oil in a heavy-bottomed frying pan, then add the sliced leek and a pinch of sea salt. Cook over low-medium heat for 10-12 minutes, or until caramelized and lightly golden. Turn off the heat.

Once the potatoes are cooked and drained, put them back in the large pot. Pour the milk over them, add the butter, and place over low heat. Mash these ingredients together with a potato masher until they are smooth and there are no lumps. Then whisk lightly through with a fork to ensure they are light and fluffy. Stir in the horseradish sauce now, if using. Season with a pinch of sea salt and plenty of black pepper to taste, then transfer to a warm serving dish and top with the caramelized leeks.

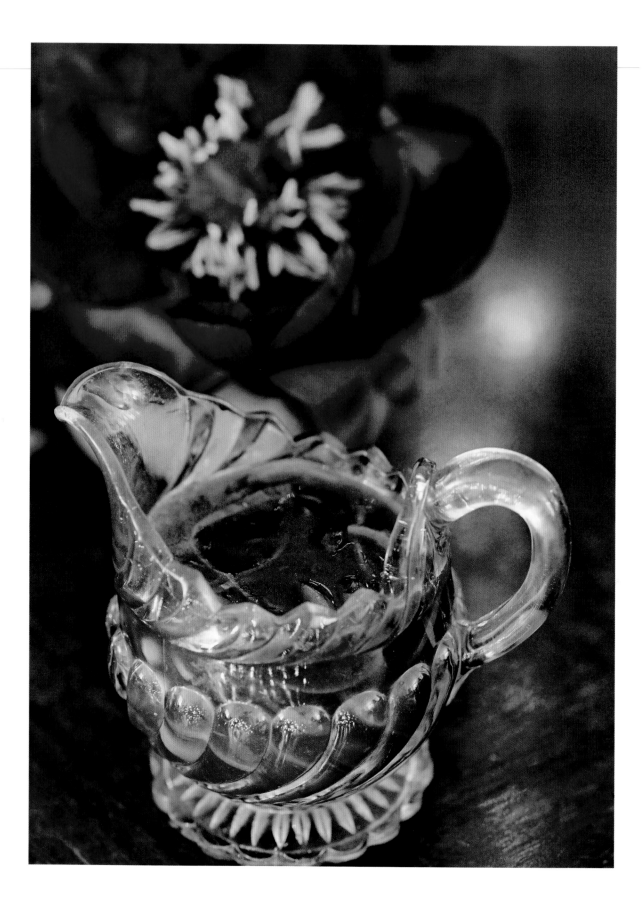

RED WINE GRAVY

SERVES 6
Prep time: 10 minutes
Cooking time: 15 minutes

INGREDIENTS

2 tablespoons light olive oil or
    vegetable oil

1 medium onion, thinly sliced

2⅛ cups mushrooms, thinly sliced

1½ tablespoons cornstarch

3⅓ cups vegetable stock
    (room temperature)

1 tablespoon chopped fresh thyme,
    or 1 teaspoon dried thyme

¾ cup red wine

¼ cup frozen peas (optional)

salt and freshly ground black pepper,
    to taste

GF, V+, DF

I absolutely love gravy and it's so easy to make. I used to buy gravy granules but this simple recipe means you never have to again. You can prepare the gravy in advance and reheat it when you're ready to eat. I often make extra, so I can freeze and then defrost it, whenever I need it. It's delicious poured over the festive roast, mashed potatoes, and roast vegetables, and, if you have some left over, it's also fantastic over mashed potatoes with veggie sausages the next day. The list goes on . . .

METHOD

Heat the oil in a medium saucepan and then sauté the onion and mushrooms for 5 minutes until softened. Mix the cornstarch into the onion and mushroom mix and then gradually pour in the vegetable stock, stirring all the time with a wooden spoon to avoid lumps.

Add the thyme and red wine and cook for 7–10 minutes on a gentle simmer, stirring often, until the gravy has thickened. You want it to be thick enough to coat the back of the spoon.

Add the frozen peas, if using, then cook for one more minute. Season with salt and pepper to taste, before serving.

CHOCOLATE AND CHERRY ROULADE

SERVES 6

Prep time: 20 minutes

Cooling time: 20–30 minutes

Cooking time: 12 minutes

INGREDIENTS

For the base:

vegetable oil, for greasing the pan

6 large free range eggs, separated

¾ cup superfine sugar

½ cup cocoa powder, sifted, plus more for dusting the pan

2 tablespoons cherry brandy, for drizzling over the base (optional)

For the filling:

1¼ cups heavy cream

2 teaspoons vanilla extract

½ cup good-quality cherry jam (St. Dalfour is good as it's made with natural fruit sugars)

15½ ounces canned pitted black cherries, drained (or cherries soaked in Kirsch if you want a more boozy dessert)

For the topping:

1 teaspoon confectioners' sugar, for dusting

2¾ ounces dark chocolate (minimum 70% cocoa solids) or milk chocolate

6 tablespoons milk or half and half

This dessert looks simply stunning with all of its chocolate creaminess, and the cherries add extra juiciness. If you don't have, or don't want to use cherries, you can make this your own way, substituting fresh berries of your choice, or chopped pecan nuts, or even milk chocolate chips. Once again, it's about a creating a festive centerpiece, a real showoff dessert. If you're making this just for adults, then it's nice to use cherries soaked in Kirsch for that extra kick. If I'm making this for children, I leave out the brandy.

METHOD

Preheat the oven to 350°F. Lightly grease a 13 x 9 inch swiss roll pan, line it with parchment paper, then brush the paper with oil and dust with cocoa powder.

First make the base. Add the sugar to the egg yolks in a medium bowl, and beat together until pale and creamy. Mix in the cocoa powder.

In a second bowl, whisk the egg whites together with a clean electric whisk until they form stiff peaks. Add 1 tablespoon of the whipped egg whites to the cocoa mixture, to loosen the consistency, then gently fold in the rest of the whites with a metal spoon, until evenly mixed, being careful not to knock out the bubbles. Pour into the prepared pan, level the surface, and bake for 12 minutes, or until the top is springy to the touch—do not overcook or the base will be too dry.

If using cherry brandy, sprinkle it evenly over the sponge base. Soak a clean dish towel in cold water and wring it out until almost dry, then place over the cooked sponge in the baking pan (this helps to keep the sponge soft) and let the sponge cool for 20-30 minutes. Meanwhile, make the filling. Whip the cream until it is just firm and holds its shape, then mix in the vanilla extract.

Turn out the sponge onto the damp dish towel on a clean work surface. Now gently peel away the parchment paper. Spread the cherry jam over the base of the sponge, then spoon the whipped cream evenly over the jam, spreading it with a knife (leaving a

¾-inch gap around the edge). Dot with the cherries (or other berries of your choice, or chopped nuts, or milk chocolate chips).

Now roll up your sponge. Lift the dish towel and tuck under the front edges and start to roll carefully, using the dish towel to help you lift and roll the chocolate base in on itself. Using two large spatulas, carefully transfer the roulade onto a serving plate. Use a sieve to dust the top with confectioners' sugar. Melt the dark chocolate and the milk (or cream) together in a heatproof bowl, and set over a pan of simmering water, until it becomes a well-blended, smooth chocolate sauce.

Drizzle the sauce over the roulade and store in a cool place until ready to serve.

WEIGHT

Ounces (oz)	Grams (g)
½	15
1	25
1½	45
2	55
2½	70
3	85
4	115
5	140
6	170
7	200
8	225
12	340
1lb	455
1lb 8oz	680
2lb	910

LIQUIDS

Fl.oz (pints)	Milliliters (liters)
2	60
3	90
4	120
5 (¼ pint)	140
6	180
7	205
8	230
10 (½ pint)	290
12	340
14	400
15	430
20 (1 pint)	570
2 pints	1.1 L
1 tablespoon	(½ fl.oz/15ml)
2 tablespoons	(1 fl.oz/30ml)
3 tablespoons	(1½ fl.oz/45ml)
4 tablespoons	(2 fl.oz/60ml)
6 tablespoons	(3 fl.oz/85ml)
8 tablespoons	(4 fl.oz/115ml)

OVEN TEMPERATURES

°F	°C
275	135
300	150
325	160
350	180
375	190
400	200
425	220